PRAISE FOR *THE OTHER TALK*

"With vulnerability, honesty, and humility, Kiely offers an invitation for white youth to examine the history of racism in the United States of America and its impact on their own identity and relationships. These pages unpack what it means to be an ally, what it means to listen, what it means to grow. There have been many calls to action, *The Other Talk* is a mighty, necessary response."

—RENÉE WATSON, Newbery Honor recipient and Coretta Scott King Award–Winning author of *Love Is a Revolution*

"Honest. Raw. Necessary. *The Other Talk* is required reading. A nuanced examination of the constructs of race and the insidious, pervasive roots of white privilege in the United States, *The Other Talk* is a clarion call to action, a call to love, to do better for ourselves, our neighbors, and our nation. Brendan Kiely challenges the reader to sit with their discomfort—believe me there are uncomfortable moments in any real discussion about race—and to learn through the radical act of listening and questioning lies that have passed for too long as truths. Kiely dares us to imagine a better country and then to step up to make that place real."

—SAMIRA AHMED, *New York Times* bestselling author of *Internment*

"In *The Other Talk*, Brendan Kiely reflects on personal experience, history, and current events to speak the truth about white privilege and racism with vulnerability, nuance, compassion, and hope. An urgent call for white teens to listen, reflect, speak up, and join the fight for justice."

—RANDY RIBAY, author of the National Book Award finalist *Patron Saints of Nothing*

"There are books you buy to keep and there are books you buy to immediately give to others to read. This is the book you want everyone else to read because it is so important. Kiely writes his truths in such a compassionate and accessible manner that he invites readers to enter the difficult conversation of race without blame and instead to focus on the necessary conversations that need to be had for real change to happen. I'm so glad he wrote this book."

—ELLEN OH, author of *Finding Junie Kim* and cofounder of We Need Diverse Books

"Can a nonfiction book about race be a heart-pounding page-turner? *The Other Talk* sure is. Kiely's conversational style draws you right in, and his honesty about his own mistakes and misconceptions (wow, did he make a lot of mistakes!) will make you laugh, cringe, and grow. If you're a white person who thinks a lot about race, you should read this book. If you're a white person who doesn't think a lot about race, you should read this book. You'll be very glad you did."

—ADAM GIDWITZ, bestselling author of the Newbery honoree *The Inquisitor's Tale*

"An unflinching reckoning with white privilege, Kiely places his life on the examination table, dissecting his own past to show how systemic racism infects us all. *The Other Talk* invites readers to an honest conversation that is uncomfortable, messy, and absolutely necessary."

—MINH LÊ, early care and education policy expert and
critically acclaimed author of *Drawn Together*

"This book gets right to the heart of the white impulse to imagine that we are exceptional. It contains facts, feeling, and the kind of candor that challenges young people at the door, but also welcomes them inside. We need more white people talking honestly to other white people about what whiteness means and how it works. Let's talk about guilt versus responsibility. Let's talk about denial. Let's talk about Brendan Kiely's *The Other Talk*."

—OLIVIA A. COLE, critically acclaimed author of
The Truth about White Lies

"Accessible and timely. It's time for white people to talk to each other about racism, and this book is a great first step."

—JULIE MURPHY, #1 *New York Times* bestselling
author of the Dumplin' series

"As awareness and public dialogue about systemic racism have increased, many have scrambled for resources in well-intentioned efforts to learn and change. Yet, no amount of reading can dismantle systems of oppression without action. This is the book for all the white folks who asked, 'How do I talk to my kids/students about racism?' *The Other Talk* provides a blueprint not only of the key points necessary to build a foundation of anti-racist, critical consciousness, it also models the *how* of these necessary conversations in white spaces. Through deeply personal stories woven with historical facts and racial statistics shared in conversational, engaging language, Brendan Kiely peels back layers of white privilege and pushes other white folks to take on the responsibility of whiteness and dismantling systemic racism."

—**JOANNA HO,** *New York Times* **bestselling author of**
Eyes that Kiss in the Corners

"Compelling, riveting, emotionally stirring—Brendan Kiely gives us a critical tool for consciousness raising and freedom dreaming. Read this, then read it again, then talk about it with those you know and love."

—**JULIA TORRES, nationally acclaimed educator,**
scholar, and librarian

"*The Other Talk* is the conversation that white people should have had with each other long ago. This book is *long overdue*. For those who have been unable to confront the truth about what whiteness is and how it is lived, Brendan Kiely offers a supportive, accessible, and necessary late pass. This book is not just an opportunity to school yourself. It is a rare chance to truly free yourself."

—**CORNELIUS MINOR, nationally renowned educator**
and author of *We Got This: Equity, Access,* **and**
the *Quest to Be Who Our Students Need Us to Be*

"For all of us who have wrestled with our own whiteness and have asked, what can I do about racial injustice? This is the book we've been waiting for. Teachers, young people, their families, and school communities will find hope and humility in Brendan's book. It offers us practical ways to talk with each other about and move beyond the fear that paralyzes us in doing this work, and it gives us the strength of a larger community committed to having this other talk."

—SARAH FLEMING, PhD, educator and scholar

"Brendan tells the truth. It is as simple as that—and as complicated. In my twenty years of teaching youth about whiteness and white privilege, I have often found it challenging to be honest with myself and my students without being met with resistance, frustration, and, sometimes, anger. Brendan offers us a way into *The Other Talk* with grace, patience, honesty, and vulnerability."

—KEITH NEWVINE, assistant professor of literacy, SUNY Cortland

Also by Brendan Kiely

All American Boys (with Jason Reynolds)
The Gospel of Winter
The Last True Love Story
Tradition

the OTHER ta!k

reckoning with
~~my~~ OUR white privilege

Brendan Kiely

atheneum

A Caitlyn Dlouhy Book

NEW YORK LONDON TORONTO SYDNEY NEW DELHI

$$\mathcal{A}$$

atheneum

An imprint of Simon & Schuster Children's Publishing Division • 1230 Avenue of the Americas, New York, New York 10020 • The names and identifying details of some individuals have been changed. • Text © 2021 by Brendan Kiely • Jacket illustration © 2021 by Sean Williams • Jacket design by Dan Potash © 2021 by Simon & Schuster, Inc. • Photogram on p. 79 courtesy Karl Davies (karldavies.co.uk). Every effort has been made to correctly acknowledge and contact the source and/or copyright holder of this image. Simon & Schuster apologizes for any unintentional errors or omissions, which will be corrected in future printings of this book. • All rights reserved, including the right of reproduction in whole or in part in any form. • Atheneum logo is a trademark of Simon & Schuster, Inc. • For information about special discounts for bulk purchases, please contact Simon & Schuster Special Sales at 1-866-506-1949 or business@simonandschuster.com. • The Simon & Schuster Speakers Bureau can bring authors to your live event. For more information or to book an event, contact the Simon & Schuster Speakers Bureau at 1-866-248-3049 or visit our website at www.simonspeakers.com. • Interior design by Dan Potash • The text for this book was set in Iowan Old Style. • Manufactured in the United States of America • First Edition • 2 4 6 8 10 9 7 5 3 1 • Library of Congress Cataloging-in-Publication Data •Names: Kiely, Brendan, 1977– author. • Title: The other talk : a reckoning with our white privilege / Brendan Kiely. • Description: First edition. | New York : Atheneum, an imprint of Simon & Schuster Children's Publishing Division, [2021]. | "A Caitlyn Dlouhy Book." | Audience: Ages 12 up. | Summary: "Most kids of color grow up talking about racism. They have "The Talk" with their families—the honest talk about survival in a racist world. But white kids don't. They're barely spoken to about race at all—and that needs to change. Because not talking about racism doesn't make it go away. Not talking about white privilege doesn't mean it doesn't exist. The Other Talk begins this much-needed conversation for white kids. In an instantly readable and deeply honest account of his own life, Brendan Kiely offers young readers a way to understand one's own white privilege and why allyship is so vital, so that we can all start doing our part—today."—Provided by publisher. • Identifiers: LCCN 2021018958 (print) | LCCN 2021018959 (ebook) | ISBN 9781534494046 (hardcover) | ISBN 9781534494053 (paperback) | ISBN 9781534494060 (ebook) • Subjects: LCSH: Kiely, Brendan, 1977—Juvenile literature. | Whites—Race identity—United States—Juvenile literature. | Racism—United States—Juvenile literature. | Whites—United States—Social conditions—Juvenile literature. | Blacks—Race identity—United States—Juvenile literature. | African Americans—Social conditions—Juvenile literature. | Social justice—United States—Juvenile literature. • Classification: LCC E184.A1 K444 2021 (print) | LCC E184.A1 (ebook) | DDC 305.809/073—dc23 • LC record available at https://lccn.loc.gov/2021018958 • LC ebook record available at https://lccn.loc.gov/2021018959

For Finn.
Son, we have a lot to talk about—
including all that you'll teach me.

And for my father.
Dad, thank you for having
this talk with me after all.

Contents

	An Introduction by Jason Reynolds	xv
1.	Bottle of Nesquik, Bottle of Long Since Forgotten	1
2.	Two Americas	7
3.	So What Is This Talk I Never Got?	17
4.	How I Tell a Story	25
5.	White Boy	37
6.	Chicken-and-Egg Problem . . . Solved!	51
7.	Cheating to Win	62
8.	History Lives in the Present	71
9.	The Entire System Is Rigged	83
10.	Ninja Runs	97
11.	Hard Look in the Mirror	114
	Interruption	124
12.	What Bullying Looks Like . . . to a Whole Community	132
13.	So Step Up!	146
14.	Well, Actually, Hang on a Second . . . Step Back	148
15.	Messing Up	153
16.	Messing Up . . . and Listening	161
17.	Who?	167
18.	Listening . . . without Getting Defensive	168
19.	Listening . . . and Believing	178
20.	Taking Action	196
	Author's Note	219
	Acknowledgments	223
	Endnotes	227
	Some People I Listened to and Learned from Who Influenced the Writing of This Book	249

Why don't white people think
they have racial identity?

—Reni Eddo-Lodge

An Introduction by Jason Reynolds

When my little cousin was young, he was a stumblebum. A klutz. But not because he was a naturally uncoordinated kid tripping on air, but because whenever he was wearing shoes, it was a guarantee that one of them would be untied. A worn booby trap. Of course, every time he hit the ground—and he hit the ground often—every adult in the vicinity would preach about how he needed to tie his shoes. They'd scold him about how he needed to pay more attention to what he was doing, where he was going, and to the two things attached to him that could make walking a dangerous activity—his sneakers. This never worked. From what I remember, my cousin never took the advice of anyone, never decided to double-knot or trade his everyday kicks in for slip-ons. It was almost like he was comfortable with falling.

I haven't seen him in a while, but it wouldn't surprise me if at this very moment, he's picking his twentysomething-year-old body up off the ground, and there's some sweet old lady walking by telling him, for the millionth time, to tie his shoes. I hope not. But thinking back on it all, I wonder why he wouldn't just do it. Like, why wouldn't my cousin just take a second, squat down, make bunny ears, and save himself from all the embarrassment? Well, my theory is that either he:

1. didn't care,
2. didn't know they'd come untied,
3. didn't know how to tie his shoes, or
4. didn't believe laces, which are nothing but fancy pieces of string, had the power to topple him.

Honestly, I don't know what the answer is, or what it was back then, and his reasoning doesn't really matter because the outcome never changed; he kept tripping, which meant he kept falling and hurting himself, and he often would fall into other people and hurt them, too.

That's pretty much what this book is about: shoes. I'm kidding. It's not about shoes at all, but it is about thinking of racism as a loose lace that white people, at some point—now would be nice!—have to tie. Sure, maybe some folks just don't care. But we know that's not you. You've already opened this book. You've already taken a step to have *The Other Talk*.

Perhaps some don't know. That's a real thing, and I get it. We are all learning about the things attached to us, making forward movement far more dangerous than it has to be. This book is simply asking you to stop for a moment. Check yourself in the mirror. Not just your shirt and pants, the big things everyone can see. Check your feet. Those shoes you push your toes into every day, the ones that have bent and molded to you so much so that you don't even think about them anymore, like skin. Are the laces (that contain your biases) tied? Tightly?

Or maybe some folks don't know how to tie their shoes. How to actually address what has come undone. I understand that, too. And I don't know if anyone has all the answers. But this book is meant to at least show how it's a process. And it takes practice. And patience. And the desire to get it right.

And then there are the folks who believe that a lace doesn't have enough weight to get in the way of walking. It's not like it's a jagged crack in the sidewalk, or a tree root sticking out the ground, right? Well . . . wrong. And that, my friends, might be the most important goal of my brother Brendan Kiely's work. Not only can a thin lace of racism tangle you up and put you in a situation where you might hurt yourself, it will also put you in a situation where you'll hurt others, break another person's bones, scar another person's knee, make another person the subject of unwanted attention and judgment.

Get it?

Now, there are lots of different ways I could've introduced this book. Tons of stories I could've told. Stories about moments in my life where racism made me feel small, or broken, or angry, or or or. I could've even spilled about me and Brendan's friendship and how we've traveled the country together, and all the drama that ensued from people who believe racism isn't an appropriate conversation to have with young folks. But . . . nah. I mean, you know those stories. You've heard some of them or have seen them on the internet and television, even if it's to the tune of someone saying none of it exists. Even if it's to the tune of *Black people are the problem*. I have to believe—I *have* to believe—you've heard something about racism in America. And because I know you've heard some of the sad narratives attached to it, I decided to leave that out of all this. I mean, you don't need to hear about pain to care, do you? Of course not. So I figured it'd be better to just talk about my awkward cousin. One, because . . . well . . . he's a trip! Get it? A . . . trip! Sorry, I couldn't resist. But also because he isn't who we think of in these discussions. He isn't who we hear about or who we fight over or argue about—the goofball bopping down the street, minding his business.

But the thing about him, and why he's so important to this framework, is that there was always something in the way. Something he didn't see, or didn't care about, or didn't know how to fix, or didn't think would matter, and so his joy—his natural joy—would be cut short over and over again. It's not always stories about police sirens and white sheets. It's not always slurs and blood. Sometimes, for me, the most critical thing to do when dealing with such a big, complicated topic like race is to avoid the explosions and whittle it all down to just a story about my little cousin. Questions about my family and all the untied laces.

Because, well, he . . . is you.

And you are my family, too.

1

Bottle of Nesquik, Bottle of Long Since Forgotten

Here's the situation:

Two teenagers go to a convenience store.

Actually, two different convenience stores.

Kid A is in a car that pulls up outside one at a gas station in Jacksonville, Florida. Music's bumping. Got "Beef" by Lil Reese, Lil Durk, and Fredo Santana cued up on the playlist.

Kid B walks into one on a busy street near Boston, Massachusetts. Headphones on. Head bobbing to A Tribe Called Quest's "Can I Kick It?" *Yes you can,* he mouths along as he pulls open the glass door.

Kid A's there with three friends. One of them goes into the store to grab some snacks and a bottle of something long since forgotten.

Kid B's there to get a bottle of Strawberry Nesquik.

They're just two kids, two kids loving their music and going to the convenience store—but then everything changes.

Kid A's waiting in the car. "Beef" blasting. He's out with friends. They're having a good time.

Kid B, though, grabs his bright yellow bottle of Nesquik and slips it into the folds of his puffy down coat. *Yes you can!* Then he strolls right out the door without looking back. He hasn't paid for the Strawberry Nesquik. He's stolen it. And he's done this before. He's got a crush on a girl who loves Strawberry Nesquik (even though it's gross—and it *is*—it's gross!), and he loves giving her a bottle in the hallway before homeroom because he likes the coconut smell of her hair and the way her high-sprayed bangs rise off her forehead like a flag. He likes the way roller coasters run wild loops through his gut whenever their eyes meet. He gives her one of these stolen bottles of Strawberry Nesquik about once a week, maybe more, and he's been doing it for the past month.

He hasn't thought twice about the people in the store.

Or anybody else, really.

Just the girl with the bangs climbing toward the sky.

More than one thousand miles south on Route 95, Kid A's bumping to the music with his buddies, still waiting for the friend in the store, when a car pulls up beside them. The two adults in the car start giving the friends dirty looks. The clock starts ticking. In three and half minutes everything will be different. Lives will have changed. But when the car pulls up, Kid A has no idea. All he sees are the scowls. Scowls he's seen before. He's not doing anything wrong. He's just a kid and his music is loud. And if the adults would just take a breath and let it go, let this boy be a kid and let his too-loud music thump, only a few minutes later his car would be gone, the music would be gone, and there'd be no story to tell.

Instead, the woman in the car opens her door, and before she leaves to go into the store, the man who's with her turns to her and says, "I hate this thug music." This man, the scowler, starts yelling at Kid A and his friends, starts calling them names. One of Kid A's friends turns down the music, but Kid A's sick of the scowler's scowls. Sick of the way this man, this adult, keeps talking to him, so he turns the music back up and tries to drown him out. Tries to drown out everything the man's saying. Those scowls. Those kinds of arguments. He's all too used to them. He's heard it all before, and all too often, he's heard the slurs and the name-calling that follows. He's heard it all before and he's heard it enough—so up goes the music, bass rattling the car doors. Up goes his voice too, yelling back at the man, matching him insult for insult. But the clock is still ticking.

The clock is still ticking when Kid A's friend comes out of

the convenience store and gets back in the car. The clock's still ticking as Kid A and the man keep yelling, their voices loud enough to climb up and over the music. The clock's still ticking when the adult man shouts at Kid A, "You aren't going to talk to me like that."

And it's supposed to be kids driving around through the night, shouting their lyrics—*In the field, we play for keeps/I'm out here, no hide-and-seek*—like kids all over the country do, are doing, will do later. The clock is still ticking when the man reaches into his glove compartment and pulls out a 9 mm pistol—and then everything goes into hyperspeed.

He fires.

The man fires and fires. Bullets crash through the door beside Kid A. Bullets rip through the car around and into Kid A. Bullets explode and crack open the night as the kids throw the car into reverse, try to escape, but the man steps out of his own car, crouches in a shooting stance, and fires and fires and fires. Ten bullets in all.

The clock only stops ticking when the kids pull into a nearby parking lot and find Kid A gasping for air. Losing his breath. No chance to drink that bottle of who-knows-what soda or whatever as his blood spills across the car seats, down onto the concrete, where it stains the parking lot, the whole town, the whole state, the whole country, because Kid A's blood is the blood of another innocent, unarmed child who has been called names, called all kinds of things, like a thug, and who hasn't done anything illegal, hasn't done anything wrong, except be a kid—and murdered all the same.

+ + +

Kid B's the one who did something wrong. Kid B's the one who did something illegal. Kid B's the actual thief.

But nobody's ever called him one. Nobody knows he *is* one. Because nobody's ever even suspected he's one.

In fact, later that spring, when Kid B is working for a talent agency in Boston, auditioning to model for a series of magazine ads, the casting director will lean forward and say to Kid B, "Hey, yeah, we definitely want you. You look like the kid next door. You look like the all-American boy."

Now let me tell you more about Kid A.

He was someone's son. He liked Jacksonville, where he lived. He liked to play basketball and PlayStation. But his singular passion was music. All the music. *In the field, we play for keeps* . . . Making mixes for his buddies. He had dreams and family and friends.

You might say he was just another "all-American boy," except I fear not enough people told him that. The adults who pulled up in the car beside him certainly didn't. That man took one look at Kid A and *suspected* . . . *assumed* . . . *profiled* Kid A as a "thug." As someone who was up to no good. Even though he wasn't. The man prejudged Kid A—and his *prejudice* did all the thinking. And Kid A paid the price for it.

But Kid A wasn't a thug. He wasn't a thief.

Kid B was the thief. The way Kid B acted, you might call him the thug.

But here's what else I have to tell you:

Kid A was Black.

And Kid A was a real person. His name was Jordan Davis.

And Jordan Davis was murdered because of racial prejudice—because of racism.

Kid B was white.

And Kid B was a real person too. That kid? He's me. Brendan Kiely. I'm the thief.

And I'm alive because . . . well, we're going to get to all that.

Two Americas

You know how I said Jordan Davis had dreams, a passion for music?

Well, that same spring day that I was walking into the corner store near where I lived, the music I was listening to was instilling in me a passion for words. I loved those lyrics, those words—and I was dreaming about one day working with words. I loved rap music. I loved hip-hop. All of it was poetry—so I loved poetry—and I liked playing with words so that the sounds bounced around like tiny basketballs in my mouth. I didn't care about English class, but I loved playing with words, and I knew that when I grew up, I wanted to somehow work with them.

And, unlike Jordan Davis, I got to live my dream.

Flash-forward a lot of years. I mean A LOT of years . . .

Kid B (me) publishes his first novel. Woo-hoo! I was so psyched! I mean, honestly, I worked on trying to publish a novel for ten years (*ten years!*) and it was finally happening. And at the same exact time, in the same exact month, in the same exact year, another guy—who'd also been working for ten years (*ten years!*) to try to publish a novel—was publishing his first novel.

And so for both of us, after all that hard work—wham!

Holy @#&%?! It was happening!

But what was even cooler than that was that we were both being published by the same company. Why'd that make it even cooler? Because they put us on the road to promote our books together. Now, this guy happens to be Jason Reynolds. (Uh, yes, who also kindly wrote the introduction to this book.) And while we were out there on the road together, we really had no idea what the heck we were doing. We were mostly hanging out in empty bookstores and libraries and whatnot, but we didn't care—we were just so grateful and excited to be there. And while we were traveling, he and I were becoming friends. This is important for a number of reasons.

One, I love this guy. He's now one of my closest friends.

But *one and a half*: as we were becoming friends, something strange was starting to dawn on me.

Because *two*, the more we traveled, the more it occurred to me that even though we were traveling to the same cities, walking side by side through the same airports, the same hotel lobbies, bookstores, and school hallways, he, a Black man, and I, a white man, were having very different experiences.

It was impossible for me not to notice the pileup of racist stuff that kept happening no matter where we were or who we were with. I mean the extra and excessive pat-downs at airport security. I mean the front-desk clerks at hotels and the front-office administrators at schools giving suspicious looks when we walked in the door. I mean the way people spoke at the coffee shop or in a restaurant. Not to me. Never to me. To Jason. That's how deep racism lives in so many people. It sits behind the eyes in their glances. It whispers beneath the words in their tone of voice. And it was stretched out like the night sky, lying lower and closer than I ever thought across the entire country.

And when it's just sitting there like that, sometimes it flares up even more blatantly.

One time Jason and I walked into a bank together in Washington, DC. Two authors walk into a bank—it sounds like the first line of a really bad dad joke, except what happened wasn't funny at all.

Jason was the customer of the bank. He went up to the teller to do the business he had to do, and the teller said, "For a transaction like that, I have to get the manager." She went around back to get him. Jason and I waited. The manager of the bank came out into the lobby; he was a white man, just like me. And as he walked toward us, he walked right past Jason, stuck his hand out to me, another white man, and said, "Hey, how can I help you, sir?"

I was livid. I explained that it wasn't me he was supposed to help. I remained mad as they foisted some poor salesman on me as the bank manager tried miserably to prove he hadn't done what he'd just done. I was still angry when Jason and I got into a cab later, and when I told Jason how mad I was, he just shook his head and said he'd already let it go.

"If I got mad every time something like that happened to me," he said, "I'd be mad all day."

I had to take a breath. I didn't know what to say after that. I was still angry, and I didn't know what made me angrier: that what had happened at the bank had just happened, or that Jason was so used to it, he'd grown calluses around his heart to protect his emotions.

Now, okay. Were we also having a great time? Yes. Were there all kinds of great things happening for Jason as well as for me? Yes. Was there so much to celebrate and laugh about and be proud of as we traveled the country? Absolutely yes.

But everything else was happening too, all that racist stuff, and for me to ignore that, or pretend that also wasn't happening, would have been a very different kind of callus around my heart. Because I didn't get those glances at the front desks. I didn't get that tone of voice at the coffee shop. I didn't get blown off and dismissed at the bank. But I'm white—and so were most of those people doing all those things I just mentioned. I witnessed with my own eyes these two different reactions to Jason and me more times than I can count. But the one moment in particular that really stuck with me didn't have to do with any of those people. It had to do with our families—phone calls with our mothers.

And those phone calls still haunt me to this day.

Now, first you need to know that Jason and I were traveling the country together in the spring of 2014. That's important because that was shortly after George Zimmerman was acquitted in the murder trial of Trayvon Martin. In case you don't know, Trayvon Martin was a seventeen-year-old Black boy who was shot and killed by an older man, George Zimmerman, in Florida in early 2012. The subsequent court case took a long time, and in July 2013, Zimmerman was acquitted—basically, he was found "not guilty" of murder, so he could go free. He was acquitted because there's a law in Florida that's commonly known as "stand your ground." What this means is, you can shoot somebody in self-defense and it's not a crime. Which is scary to think about. Because if you claim self-defense and no one else but the shot person was there, who's to say if you're lying or not?

Well, no one.

So—back to the phone calls.

While we're traveling around the country together, Jason's mother calls him. A Black woman, who, as I've heard him describe, was from South Carolina and who has the psychological, emotional, and physical scars from Jim Crow racism in America. And she calls Jason to say, essentially, "I'm scared for your life, son. I'm terrified there might be a George Zimmerman out there for you."

What an awful thing for a mother to have to say.

What an awful thing for a mother to have to *feel*.

And what an awful thing for Jason, her child, to have to say what he said next: "Ma, don't worry about it. I'm going to be okay. I'm going to be okay. I'm going to be okay." What an awful thing for him to have to reassure her that he can travel around the country because he has to for his job and that it's all going to be okay.

But then it occurred to me.

Did my mother call me? Did my mother call me to say, *Hey, Brendan, I'm terrified for your life?*

Nope.

Now, my mother loves me, okay? I'm very grateful. And I love you too, Ma! But it would never occur to her to be afraid for me in this way. She wouldn't have cause to have that same fear that Jason's mother has.

Are you following me?

Because as we're traveling around the country, we're supposed to be living out our dreams here. We were, in fact, living out our dreams in many ways. But neither could we escape the fact that, as we were traveling around the country, we were the living embodiment of Dr. Martin Luther King Jr.'s description of two Americas living side by side.

"There are two Americas," Dr. King said way back in 1968—and it was all too clear how true that still was as Jason and I were traveling the country together in 2014.

Two different Americas in the airports.

Two different Americas in the hotels.

Two different Americas in the schools.

Two different Americas for our mothers.

Two different Americas for him and me.

Just like the two different Americas for me and Jordan Davis.

Two different Americas, divided by racism. And those two Americas exist whether you are in Jacksonville, Boston, Baton Rouge, Madison, Albuquerque, New York, Orlando, Anchorage, or anywhere else in the country. It's not a Black and white divide—it's a racism divide, so it affects everybody: People of South and Central American descent. People of Mexican descent. People of Middle Eastern descent. Of South, Central, and East Asian descent. Alaska Natives. Indigenous people living in the United States. People of Pacific Islander descent. Black families who emigrated from Africa or the Caribbean or elsewhere. Black families descended from people who were brought to this country against their will or born in this country in slavery.

So, so many people of the Global Majority* living in the United States.

---

* **The one and only footnote in the entire book!!!**
In this book, I'm trying to be as specific as possible and honor the way people identify racially and culturally. And even though I am writing about white privilege and white racial identity—which (necessarily) centers on whiteness—for the purposes of examination and awareness, when I refer to large groups of people that include Black people, Indigenous people, Latinx people, people of Asian descent, and all people who are often grouped together under the term "people of color" or BIPOC, I've chosen to use the term "the Global Majority." I was inspired by my reading of Tiffany Jewell's *This Book Is Anti-Racist*, where she, and many others involved with Montessori for Social Justice, explain that this term is more empowering and has nothing to do with "whiteness" or "color"—rather, it is a term that honors the power, magnitude, and overall ubiquity of people who do not identify as "white" across the whole planet.

And, yes, racism affects people who identify as white in the United States as well, wherever they might be from—*but in a very different way*, and we're going to get to all of this.

And since those two different Americas are everywhere, racism affects everything in our daily lives.

Because:

Racism affects our life in schools.

On public transportation.

In the kind of food we have access to.

In the homes and neighborhoods we live in.

Racism affects the kind of healthcare we get, the kinds of jobs we get interviews for . . . You get the point.

It's freaking everywhere.

And it divides.

Racism divides so that there is one America experienced by Black people, Indigenous people, and most people of the Global Majority, and there is another privileged America experienced by white people. And for white people like me, it's all too common that we don't talk much to one another about what it actually means to experience life in America *as a white person*. About the privileges we experience in our America.

In other words, although many of us talk about racism, we just don't talk about *being* white and all the privileges we get *because* we're white. All the things we don't have to worry about or contend with, because we are white. White privilege. The privileges that come with being born white.

I'm not saying those privileges are a good thing. I'm saying they're an unfair thing. And *that's* what we need to talk about.

But maybe it's not just racism we have a hard time talking about. Maybe it's "race" in general. I remember this one time when I was in middle school. I was standing on the sidewalk outside a grocery store, and I heard two adult white women talking, just gossiping about things going on in town.

"Did you see the new girl they hired at the bank?" one woman asked the other. Then she leaned closer to the other woman and said in a hushed voice, "Well, you know, she's Black."

What the heck? Why did she whisper "Black"?

Oh, Brendan, you might say, *but that was YEARS ago.* (Well, even though this incident sounds like it was from 1950, it was the 1990s—which probably sounds the same to you anyway because that is all sooo last century.)

But even if that did happen in the *last century*, all these years later (okay, fine, it really is a lot of years later), I'm now an author, and sometimes I speak at schools. And when I do, so often—seriously, still to this day!—when I'm up on the stage and I call myself a "white boy," it's as if some giant vacuum cleaner in the sky just sucked all the air out of the room.

Hussssssshhhhhh.

And every time I'm thinking, *What the heck?* (Again!) Why are we so afraid of just saying "Black" and "white"?

Probably because, for so many of us white people, we've been told that *talking* about race can be racist. Or we've been told that since we don't experience the pain of racism, we shouldn't talk about it. Or maybe (probably) it's that we, or the adult white people in our lives, feel so confused and uncomfortable about it all, we're hoping someone else will do all the talking about it so that we don't have to fumble and make mistakes and make fools of ourselves, because we know race and racism aren't just serious topics—they can be deadly serious topics.

I get it. I honestly do. I mean, I'm nervous as I type these words because I know I'm not going to get everything right. But I think I have to try. I think many of us white people have to try harder to have honest conversations about race and racism and what it means to be a white person experiencing another America (a privileged America) that racism divides and separates.

Because here's the thing: Black, Indigenous, and many, many families who identify with and descend from people of the Global Majority are already having these conversations with one another. *All. The. Time.*

In fact, these conversations often take the form of this thing some people call "The Talk."

A "talk" this white boy certainly never got.

(I hope the air didn't suddenly get sucked out of the room right then. Because we're just getting started, friends.)

3

So What Is This Talk I Never Got?

So maybe you're (um, white) like me?

And maybe you grew up trusting law enforcement. Maybe you believe police officers are basically the "good guys." There to protect the rest of us from the "bad guys." I did. I grew up believing that the cops were called when someone was putting the rest of us in danger in some way.

But. I grew up in an almost exclusively white community and went to almost exclusively white schools (especially when I switched to a Catholic high school).

And in many communities and families of the Global Majority, kids do not grow up feeling the same way about the police. In fact, trusting law enforcement is a lot more complicated for them. And they are made aware of this starting from a very young age—in other words, they are given "The Talk."

Most white kids don't know this, don't know what The Talk consists of, or why it's even needed.

I sure didn't know about it when I was twelve, or sixteen, or even into my twenties.

This is how it goes:

You've probably heard of George Floyd, but in case you haven't, I should tell you a little about who he was first, because it is the monstrous act that was done to him that makes families have to have The Talk in the first place.

People always said George Floyd was a charismatic, friendly, and charming guy. His employers, his friends, and most importantly, his family talked about it all the time. And when he was growing up, they called him "Big Friendly." He was already 6'6" in high school, and he became a star tight end. In fact, he helped take his team all the way to the Texas state championship game in 1992—where they played in the Houston Astrodome!

Later in life, he got into some trouble with the law—with drugs and theft—but he left Texas and moved to Minneapolis for a fresh start. He worked as a security officer for a homeless shelter run by the Salvation Army, and at various bars. He was a rapper. He worked with his church's ministry. He was the father of five children. And he was forty-six years old when he was arrested outside a convenience store for allegedly using a fake $20 bill, which shouldn't have amounted to much, but turned quickly into a tragedy. The arresting officer got George Floyd onto the ground and then brutally forced a knee on his neck for nine minutes and twenty-nine seconds, killing him.

This murder of yet another unarmed Black man by law enforcement sent ripples of cold recognition through too many families of the Global Majority across the country. In fact, it was just after George Floyd was killed that a friend of mine, who is Black, had to have his family's Talk with his eight-year-old son, who is also Black. He sat his son down to tell him about what happened to George Floyd and why he needed to tell him about it.

"I knew," my friend told me, "I'd have to hurt him a little now, to try to protect him in the long run."

The Talk began with a conversation about skin color.

And about how some people wanted to do other people, like him and some of his friends, harm because of their skin color.

And about how sometimes those people didn't even know they wanted to do harm, but that other times the people really *did* know that they wanted to do harm.

And that sometimes the people who could do harm, or the people who even wanted to do harm, were police officers.

And about how sometimes it's the way they have been trained.

And about how other times it's how they haven't been trained.

But whatever the reason, it means that sometimes they can really cause harm.

And if they do cause harm, most likely they will get away with it. They can forget about it—and forget about hurting you.

But if you get hurt, the way they hurt you will *stay* with you—my friend had to explain all this to his son.

Then he did a deep dive. He had to lay it all out, to an eight-year-old boy: How to speak to a police officer, saying "yes, sir" and "no, sir." How to hold his body. Where to put his hands. It went on and on, and when my friend was finished, he made his son repeat it all back to him. Again and again. Until his son, his eight-year-old son, was able to say it all, word for word.

But The Talk wasn't over. Next came another conversation about why my friend was so hard on his son in public, at school, in the grocery store, when the family was going out for ice cream or whatever. Because the racism that lies at the heart of those possibly deadly interactions with a police officer is the same racism that could lie at the heart of an interaction with a store clerk, a teacher, another patron in the ice-cream shop, and so on. The store clerk might incorrectly assume you are stealing something. The teacher might incorrectly assume you cheated on the test. The patron at the ice-cream shop might incorrectly assume you are fighting with your friend when you are only joking around.

"And *you*," he explained to his son, "will be the one paying the consequences for *their* mistakes."

And those consequences might affect you for a long time—might affect the way the teacher treats you for the rest of the school year or how the clerk looks at you anytime you're in the store.

Those are the dangers that lie at the heart of racism everywhere in America.

My friend said it was hard, hard to sit down with his elder son to have this talk. Particularly because his son wants to be a police officer when he grows up. There are police officers in the family. His son wants to be one of the "good guys" protecting people from "bad guys." So it broke my friend's heart to have to "watch the light in my son's eyes dim a little" as he told him why he needed to behave a specific way in public, especially with police officers. "I need to tell you this," he told his son, "and I need you to act this way, so you can come home to us."

Believe me—he did not *want* to have this talk with his son. But he had to, just like *he'd* been given a similar talk when he was growing up, only the story his father told him wasn't about a name on the news—it was about his own uncle, a Black man killed by white police officers in South Carolina. So my friend knew, if he ever had kids, he'd have to do the same as his father did. And every single one of his Black and Brown friends had been given some version of the same talk when they were kids too. The cautionary stories their families passed down to them became their own lived stories: *Oh, wait, did that cop just call me that? Am I really getting pulled over for going through a yellow light? Did he really just bust out my taillight for an excuse to stop me? Is he really asking me to get out of the car?* And as the stories they heard became their own stories, they became the stories they'd tell their own children as well. As my friend was doing now.

As too many Black families have to do. Or, in fact, as too many families of the Global Majority have to do. Because whether it is particular to the Muslim experience, or East Asian, or South Asian, or Latinx, or Indigenous, or however their family identifies, they have their own version of The Talk and how they make clear to their children the ways they can and must survive and thrive in the face of racism in America.

Because The Talk my friend gave his son really is about survival. It's about surviving racism, whether that racism is hiding in a convenience store or in a police car, or revealed in the casting decisions of the school play, or tucked between words people shout from the stands at a ball game. It's about surviving racism even when it just hangs in the air like a quietly murmuring cloud drifting from one corner of a classroom to another. The Talk—it's about survival.

And part of survival is also about pride. It's about knowing that you are Black and beautiful. It is about loving to celebrate Diwali even if your classmates don't know what it is or aren't kind when they hear about it. It is singing the song your grandmother sang in Korean, Cherokee, or Urdu. It is about calling your tío Tío, and your tía Tía, with loud, public, loving pride. Those aren't my stories, but I'm mentioning them here as a reminder to white people like me that the entire Talk isn't all negative, that it can also be about knowing that your culture should be celebrated.

So why is it that we white people aren't given a talk about what it means to be white in America? What if we *did* have a talk about being white? We need to, don't you think?

If The Talk is about survival in the face of racism, I think this "other talk," the talk for white people, also has to do with racism. But not about survival. Maybe it's more about how we *don't* have to have The Talk to survive. Instead, this "other talk" should be about being white, about white privilege. Because when it comes right down to it, they are basically the same thing:

Living as a white person *is* white privilege.

So, yes, that means this other talk is about how racism divides this country and how as white people we live in another, privileged, America. And it's about how white people can't escape living with white privilege. *And* (yes, this last one is a really important "and"!) it's also about how if we learn about that divide . . .

. . . and understand how it's worked in the past . . .

. . . so that we can recognize how it's still at work today . . .

. . . we can better figure out how to work toward more racial justice . . .

. . . by taking some responsibility for that other, privileged America . . .

. . . AND work to change it.

But before I can work to change it, I first have to know what it is, right? I mean, I keep talking about a divided America, one America, and another privileged America, right?

Well, so, in order for me to start talking about that privileged America, let me tell you about the time I got pulled over for "recklessly minivanning" it down the highway.

You were doing what?

Yeah. Exactly.

4

How I Tell a Story

Okay. Embarrassingly for me, I was the last of all my friends to get my driver's license—so, yes, I most certainly had a chip on my shoulder about that. When I finally got it, I was like, *Oh, yeah! It's my turn to drive!* Now I was that wicked cool guy (as we used to say) who shared the family minivan with his mom, but whatever, I didn't care, because one night there I was, finally getting to drive all my friends around for once. Finally!

So I'm cruising along Route 1 South, heading back home toward Boston. Bombing down the highway, driving my minivan full of white kids like me. There's a stretch of Route 1 close to where one of my buddies lived that's a speed trap. The speed limit drops from fifty-five to forty-five for a mile or so. I didn't know that at the time. And I was flooring it. Doing seventy-five miles an hour in a forty-five zone. I know, right? Who knew a minivan could go that fast? (It shouldn't. And I shouldn't have been pushing it like that—it was dumb, dangerous, and, yup, totally illegal.)

I don't know how many of you are driving yet, but you should be aware that if you're going thirty miles or more over the speed limit, it's not only speeding, it's also reckless driving. I was out there endangering lives. So no boasting here—I'm just setting the scene so you can see what happened in the end.

So as I'm minivanning it seventy-five down the highway, a police car pulls up behind me. Lights flash. Sirens wail. And I'm nervous.

But pause right there.

Because remember what I told you about The Talk and how I never got one? How nobody ever warned me that my interactions with the police could be dangerous for me—precisely because they weren't afraid my interactions with the law could be dangerous for me? All the danger, my parents, the adults in my life, assumed, would be of my own making—and in this moment that was certainly the case! But this "Talk vs. No Talk" issue, my friends, is crucial to understanding everything else I'm about to tell you. Because, again. What I'm saying is that there are *two freaking Americas*.

Soooo . . . unpause, and the story continues.

All right, I'm minivanning it down the highway at

seventy-five miles an hour, and a police car pulls up behind me. Lights flash. Sirens wail. And I'm nervous. It's the first time I've ever been pulled over, so of course I'm nervous. We're all nervous when we get caught doing something we know we're not supposed to do. But I'm not nervous for my life, right? That's a very different kind of nervous. So what do I do? What does my nervousness make me do?

I floor it! (Uh, yes. In case you're wondering, minivans *can* go over seventy-five. But *why*? Aren't they supposed to be for carting families and groups around safely?)

Anyway, I keep tearing down the highway. High-speed chase. This is freaking stupid, right?

My friends are like, "Brendan, pull over! Pull over!"

And I'm like, "I don't know where it's safe to pull over!"

Finally, up ahead, I see an empty parking lot for a restaurant. I swerve in. I take my sweet time pulling into a parking space.

What kind of moron am I? This is ridiculous. Who does this?

Well, me, apparently. I do.

And I'm telling you about my ridiculousness so you can see what I was about to get away with. Getting away with something . . . which, you'll see, is going to be a theme going forward.

The police officer finally pulls up beside me, gets out of his car, and walks over, knocking on the window. He asks me for my license and registration. "No problem, Officer," I tell him. I give him my license. But I'm so dumb, I thought the writing on the back of my license was the registration. I didn't even know what a car registration was. I'm not kidding. It'd be funny if it wasn't so pathetic. Who gave me a license, anyway?

Luckily, my friend in the passenger seat knows what the heck the registration is, and he pops open the glove compartment, digs it out, and hands it to me. I give it to the officer, who stares at me for a second, then just shakes his head in disbelief.

He goes back to his car, checks things out, and then, when he comes back to my car, he asks me to step out.

So I step out of the car.

He asks, "Have you been drinking tonight, son?"

"No, I have not."

"Have you been smoking marijuana?"

"No, I have not."

"Why the hell were you going thirty miles over the speed limit?" he yells.

And I go into a sob story . . . because I can.

"Oh, Mr. Officer, we were just trying to play mini golf and that wasn't working out, and then we were supposed to go get ice cream, but everyone's yelling in the back of the car about this and that, and I just want to go home. I just want to go home. I just want to go home."

I went on and on and on, and by the end of it—oh, yeah, you already know where this story is going—did I get a ticket? Nope. Did I get a written warning? Nope. But that's not why I'm telling you this story.

I'm telling you this story because of what the police officer said to me next, the line that, every time I think of it, every time I repeat it, every time I tell this story, catches like a little fishhook in my gut and tugs and tugs and tugs to remind me what it means to have white privilege in America.

The police officer said to me, "Go home, be safe, and keep your friends safe."

I think about that line all the time: "Go home, be safe, and keep your friends safe."

Look, I'm sure the police officer took pity on me. He saw this seventeen-year-old boy acting like a seven-year-old boy, knees knocking, about to make a little puddle between his sneakers. And I'm grateful that this police officer took pity on me. I'm grateful that he looked at me with compassion and thought, *Now, there's a kid who deserves a second chance. Now, there's a kid who's probably a good kid who won't make this mistake again.* And he was right. I have absolutely never driven like *that* ever again. I don't want to endanger my life. I don't want to endanger my friends' lives. I don't want to endanger anyone else's life on the road either. But his pity for me, his kindness toward me—that's not the whole story.

I used to tell this story all the time, but the part I left out, the part that *is* the whole rest of the story, is that I am white.

Why does that matter? you might be wondering.

Welp. Here's the thing:

When I share this story in communities that are predominantly Black or many other people of the Global Majority, there's a shock. There's a hurt. Sometimes there's a head nod, the familiar recognition of a truth I didn't know when I got pulled over that day but one that they know all too well, having witnessed and experienced those two different Americas their whole lives.

Of *course* the officer looked at me with compassion first, not suspicion. Of *course* he looked at me with pity. He didn't, in one glance, see me as a threat. He looked at me with a sense of tender care.

And *that*, my friends, is white privilege. That is why *my being white* matters in the telling of the story.

That night, after the police officer told me to go home and be safe, as I pulled away, my instinct was to say, *Wow, I can't believe I just got away with that*, which was already an admission of guilt. I knew I'd "gotten away with something."

I knew something was wrong.

Honestly, that feels to me like a metaphor for living as a white person in the United States of America. Deep down in our guts we know something is wrong and we know we've gotten away with it.

I repeated those words when I eventually told my parents about the incident, and again when I told the story to friends, and *again* when I got pulled over for a (lesser) speeding incident a few years later (still no ticket), and *yet again* another year later, when I did an illegal U-turn at an intersection. I didn't just do the U-turn right in front of a cop, so that I came nose-to-nose with the police car once I'd turned around, but I even mouthed off to the officer! And guess what? *Still no ticket.*

After all those times I said to myself, *Wow, look what I just got away with.* I just felt, well . . . *lucky.* But this isn't really telling my story correctly. Or it's not really understanding something about my life in the context of other people's lives in America—or the two Americas.

So let's exit my story for a moment. Pull up, up, up to one of those shots from outer space, where you see a map of the United States at night—cities lit up like stars smashed on the dark earth around them—and then drop down, down, down to somewhere else, where someone else was being pulled over that same night I was. On another street, in another neighborhood, the teenager being pulled over was not me. Was not white. And when he stepped out of the car, the police officer, instead of compassion or pity, felt a jolt of fear zip through his veins, and he pulled his gun . . . and fired.

Equal treatment under the law? Nope. Not even close. Want some proof?

This is real:

- Black boys and young men (ages fifteen to nineteen) are twenty-one times more likely to be shot by police than white boys and young men of the same age.

- Black people comprise about 13 percent of the total US population, but they constitute 39 percent of the people killed by police.

- Black people are nearly twice as likely as white people to die in their interactions with law enforcement.

- Indigenous people are more than three times as likely as white people to die in their interactions with law enforcement.

- In New York City in 2017, 88 percent of the people stopped and frisked by police were Black and Latinx;

only 8 percent were white. (And this was only the data the police themselves actually reported!)

- And yet white people were more likely to be found with contraband or a weapon.

- Related studies show similar "stop-and-search" results in Illinois, West Virginia, Minnesota, Texas, and Arizona. In Arizona the results show that the State Highway Patrol is 3.25 times more likely to search a stopped Indigenous person than a stopped white person.

What does all this mean? You guessed it. Race matters. It's much, much more likely that a white person will not get shot or even experience excessive use of force in interactions with police officers than people of the Global Majority. Speaking for myself, even when I've outright broken the law, I've had a pretty easy and safe time when confronted by the police.

Now, if the officer had smelled marijuana when he approached my minivan that night I was speeding, or if one of the girls with me had somehow silently signaled for help, or if the car had been stolen, sure, the officer would have had greater reason to be afraid when he asked me to step out into the parking lot. But even if any of those things had been true, the chances that I would have been shot were still far lower than if I were Indigenous or Black or Latinx. And the chances were much, much lower that I would have been beaten, harassed, called names, abused, or demeaned in any other way than if I were Black or Indigenous or most people of the Global Majority in general.

Instead, my story ended with this: "Go home, be safe, keep your friends safe."

If I choose to ignore race as a factor in my story, if I choose to ignore talking about how being white helped me in that moment, I'm choosing to ignore part of the reality of my story. It's like sticking my fingers in my ears, saying "nah nah nah nah nah," and pretending it doesn't exist. I can't do that. It *does* exist. I need to factor in race. I need to factor in being white. And when I force myself to do that—and, honestly, I'm not used to factoring race into my stories like this, because I never used to—suddenly, the way I have to tell the story changes.

Knowing this now, I think about the way I used to tell this story—or any of my stories about being pulled over by the police, for that matter—and I want to tell it a little differently. Or at least end it differently. I used to love to spin the end with as much drama and flair as I could work up: "I gotta be the luckiest guy in the world!" But, really, I wasn't—and I'm not.

I was given a pass. Because I'm white. And I got away with it—again, and again, and again.

Okay, hold on a second. Am I saying that if you're white, you'll automatically "get away with it"? No. Of course not.

But if you're white, your chances of getting away with it are the highest of anyone living in America.

So now I have to ask myself: *What other stories from my life do I need to see in this new light? How many other stories from my life have I told—ignoring race, ignoring my whiteness—that now need to be retold to include how my being white affects them?*

When I think back, I start to feel a little like I've been lying to myself. Like I've been leaving out parts of the story to make myself feel better, look better. It wasn't entirely my fault. I was never taught to think, *Well, as a white person in this situation . . .* But now I really have to wonder: *What if I did? What if I made the effort to include race—in particular, my own—in every single story I tell about my life?*

How did my being white affect how I got my first magazine gig as a child model? Got into college? Got my job as a high school teacher? How did it affect my first few jobs in book publishing before that? How did my being white affect my experience as a college student or as a high school student? As a teammate on my high school basketball team? On the cross-country road trip I took with a white friend when we were nineteen?

What about all those keg parties the cops busted up when I was in high school—when nothing happened? No consequences. Zilch.

How did my being white play a role in all those stories?

I need to find out. . . . I'm still trying to find out. But one thing I do know for sure is that I have to tell all my stories now more truthfully—by always including my whiteness and asking how it plays a role.

And I get it. It can feel weird—really weird. Hard, maybe. It can even hurt. But even if it hurts a little . . . yup, we still have to give it a try. We still have to go there.

And just to be clear: talking about being white, talking

about white privilege, isn't *anti*-white. It's just being honest. If I'm honest with myself—about being white—I can learn; I can grow. I can do better.

Because that's what I want to do: do better.

One of the ways I can do better is to actually talk about my racial identity. It's true. Remember that woman I told you about who whispered "Black" outside the grocery store? She whispered "Black," but she didn't even *say* "white," even though everyone else working at the bank she was talking about was white. Even though *she and her friend* were also white.

When I look back at my childhood, at my experiences growing up, it's kind of weird that all the white adults in my life never spoke about being white when they spoke about race. I don't blame them, exactly—it was probably what they were taught too. In fact, whenever "race" was mentioned, the white adults in my life only spoke about Black people, Indigenous people, and people of the Global Majority. No one ever said "white people"; it was as if we white people didn't have a race—or a racial identity, to be more specific.

But here's a not-so-secret secret: we do.

White people do have a racial identity. And when white people do not discuss our own racial identity—our whiteness—in the conversation about race, we're adding more fuel to the fire of racism in America. Because it's kind of impossible to talk about racism in America without talking about whiteness. No, seriously. I'm not being flippant (or mean). I'm just saying it's like talking about a tree being blown down in a storm without talking about the storm. If I'm going to talk about racism in America, I kind of have to talk about race. And if I'm talking about racial identities, white racial identity is one of the big ones to include. Like the storm, it kind of plays a big role in the tree being blown over.

But again, at least in my experience, we white people have a hard time talking about being white. Part of that is fear. Part of that is probably just misunderstanding, too. I mean, seriously, when I was growing up, if I heard the words "white" and "racial identity" in the same sentence, I'd worry someone was talking about one of those loathsome hate groups.

But like I said, all of us white people have a racial identity. All of us are a part of this group called—yup—"white people." And that doesn't make you a good person or a bad person—it just makes you a white person.

But what the heck *is* a white person?

I mean, who is white?

Actually, that question is a lot harder to answer than I once thought.

Maybe the better question is: What does it mean to be a white person?

5

White Boy

Well, I think a way to understand what it means to be a white person is to talk about what it means to *live* as a white person.

A couple years ago I was climbing into an Uber in Baton Rouge, Louisiana. I had a very early (six a.m.) flight I could not miss, and though I'd booked a seat on the four thirty shuttle from the hotel to the airport, I missed the shuttle by three minutes. I was in a total panic—I had to make that flight! The relief I felt when a driver responded via my app that he'd be able to pick me up in ten minutes washed over me like a second shower. I stood out on the sidewalk in the early-morning darkness and waited for him to arrive. There was no one on the street. I'd been at a book festival for the past two days, and I was tired and eager to get home, and so I wasn't paying attention when a pickup truck pulled up to the curb. It took me a moment to realize it was the Uber I'd called. When I figured it out, I strolled over, popped open the passenger door, and jumped in.

I landed on something hard and uncomfortable, but I was busy hunting for my seat belt, wedged in the crease of the seat, while the driver, a white guy, pulled away. He started talking immediately, and we were already down the block and on our way when I finally fished out what I'd sat on.

It was a handgun in a leather holster. I don't know my guns, so I couldn't tell you what kind it was, but I knew it was a gun as soon as my thumb touched the stippled handle. I lifted it out warily in front of me.

"Oh, sorry," the driver said casually. He grabbed it from me and dropped it in the side pocket beneath the armrest, that pocket you might stick maps in, if anybody still used them, or water bottles, or now, as I write this in the time of COVID-19, an extra mask or a sanitizer pump. I heard the gun *thunk* as it hit the empty bottom, and it rattled against the thin plastic wall of the pocket as we drove on.

A stone plunged through my belly. I'd just sat on a gun, and because I don't know anything about guns, my first thought, honestly, was: *What if that had gone off when I sat down? I'd be bleeding out in this guy's truck!* Why the hell was a gun just sitting on the passenger seat?

As if he read my mind, or could tell I'd completely stopped

breathing, the driver told me, "Keep that out for protection. Just in case. Going through some of those neighborhoods— you know what I mean—never know when you're gonna need it."

You know what I mean.

I did. Or, rather, I understood what he meant, and I felt a bolt of anger zip through me. He meant some of the Black neighborhoods not far from the hotel. He meant Black people.

I was also instantly afraid. Not for myself. Or for my safety. Or for the extent to which the rest of the ride to the airport was going to be, uh, wicked awkward as I sat two feet away from this a--hole with a gun. No, I was afraid for any one of the authors who had been at the festival with me—the ones who were Black or Asian or Latinx and who, if they'd been in my situation, would have had to sit next to this man. I couldn't stop thinking about the two women I'd spent so much of the festival with who weren't white and what it might have felt like to be one of them in this situation.

The driver had said "you know what I mean" to me con- spiratorially, with a grin cocked in the corner of his mouth, reaching out across the tight space between us, as if I'd laugh along with him and say back, *Yeah, right?* As if he immediately assumed he and I shared something the people he seemed prepared to draw this gun on did not.

True, he and I were both white. But he was wrong about everything else. I didn't agree with him, but it seemed like the absolute wrong time to get into a discussion about it. He had the harried, wild-eyed look of anyone who has to work at four thirty in the morning, but this is not a story in which I am a survivor or someone who got a lucky break. This is a story about how my being *white* made me safer in that moment than if I'd been any one of the authors at the festival who was not white.

My whiteness made me very safe that morning—any and all threat I felt emerged from my imagination, not from the reality of the situation. And why? Because my being white provided me the privilege of being completely safe in the pickup truck of a man with a gun just inches from his side. And what made me safe, exactly? That he perceived me to be "white," just as he considered himself to be.

That sounds weird, doesn't it? All this "perceiving" and "considering ourselves to be." Weren't we just two white guys sitting there?

Sort of. But it's more like we *live* as white people *because* we are *perceived to be* white. And perception can change the course of everything.

Being perceived to be white, my being white, doesn't only keep me safer in situations with law enforcement; it keeps me safer because no one is targeting me *because* I'm a white person. Whereas, as all too many Black, Indigenous, and other people of the Global Majority know, they have been targeted *specifically because* of their race. Or who they are *perceived* to be.

My whiteness was like a force field protecting me that morning with the Uber driver with a handgun—a force field someone like Vincent Chin never had the privilege of having.

Vincent Chin was a twenty-seven-year-old working in computer graphics who'd been born in the Guangdong Province of China but lived nearly his entire life in Detroit, Michigan, after he was adopted by a Chinese American couple. Although Detroit had once been one of the world's car manufacturing capitals, in 1982, when Vincent Chin was enjoying his own bachelor party, the American automotive industry was in a free-falling decline. And many Americans blamed the Japanese, because the Japanese automotive industry was booming.

The night of his bachelor party, when two white men who worked in a car manufacturing plant saw Vincent, one of the men, who'd recently lost his job, said to him: "It's because of you little mother-- that we're out of work."

Now, there are a number of racist things going on here. First of all, that white guy was blaming everyone and everything Japanese as the reason for losing his job. That, in and of itself, is totally messed up, 100 percent incorrect, and off base. It certainly wouldn't be another worker's fault. Nor would it be the fault of ANYONE who was Japanese, for that matter. But what's also racist here is that this white guy looked at Vincent, who was Chinese American, and just lumped him together with all his racist assumptions about Japanese people being to blame for him losing his job. And fueled by his twisted racism, this out-of-work white guy and his white buddy picked a fight with Vincent.

Vincent fled, but the two white men chased him. In fact, they got in their car and drove around looking for him. And when they found him, they beat him with a baseball bat so severely that Vincent died in the hospital four days later.

It was horrific—and it all happened because of how the white men racially perceived . . . profiled . . . targeted . . . and attacked Vincent.

Then it got worse.

When the two white men were caught and put on trial for murder, they were charged only with manslaughter, fined $3,000, and put on probation for three years. They didn't serve a single day in jail. Not a single day. And when asked about the extremely lenient sentencing, the judge in the case said, "These aren't the kind of men you send to jail." He went on to add, "You don't make the punishment fit the crime; you make the punishment fit the criminal." The judge didn't see—didn't perceive—those two white men who'd killed Vincent as criminals worthy of jail time.

Kin Yee, president of the Detroit Chinese Welfare Council, called the sentences "a license to kill for $3,000, provided you have a steady job or are a student and the victim is Chinese."

In other words, even though they had killed a person, the two men's whiteness benefited them. You have to wonder, if they had been Black or Latinx or Asian or Indigenous, what kind of punishment would have been "fitting"? Chances are, one a helluva lot more severe than $3,000 and three years' probation. What kind of "criminal" would the judge have seen them as if they weren't white?

This anti-Asian racism at the heart of Vincent Chin's killing is only one story in a long history of racism people from the Asian diaspora have faced in America. Just to name a few of the racist policies:

- The prejudice against Chinese workers in the late nineteenth century that fueled the Chinese Exclusion

Act of 1882, which stifled immigration from East Asian countries and, in effect, conversely promoted immigration from European countries.

- The Immigration Act of 1917, propelled by anti-Asian immigrant sentiment in the United States, that made immigration from China, the Indian subcontinent, Afghanistan, Arabia, Burma (now Myanmar), Thailand, Malaysia, Indonesia, the easternmost parts of Russia, and most Polynesian states . . . illegal!

- The racist cruelty toward Filipinos in the early twentieth century that American politicians used to justify US colonial rule over the Philippines.

- Executive Order 9066, passed during World War II, that (though it was established to provide legal means to incarcerate thousands of people in German, Italian, and Japanese communities in America) targeted approximately 112,000 people of Japanese ancestry in the United States. The order was supposedly passed as a wartime measure, but it followed a tradition of racist laws that already prevented many Asian Americans from owning land, voting, and testifying against white people in court.

And those are just the racist policies! It's literally impossible to gauge the sheer magnitude of racist attitudes and interactions that pushed these policies into law—*and* what these laws and policies further reinforced or even inspired in communities across the country. It's like trying to count the branches of an enormous tree. Sure, maybe you can count some of the big ones, but once you start trying to count all the little ones that just seem to blend together into one thick net of sticks, you realize they are innumerable.

That tide of anti-Asian hate continued in the rage against the Japanese auto industry in the 1980s and '90s and in the racism Chinese and Filipino healthcare workers faced after the SARS epidemic in the 2000s. And it continued against people of East Asian descent in 2020 and 2021 after Donald Trump, while president of the United States, dangerously— and racistly—labeled COVID-19 the "Chinese virus" and the "kung flu," after which, vigilantes attacked people from all over the East Asian diaspora in the United States, making Asian American women twice as likely to suffer hate incidents, and with a particular hatefulness and cruelty that specifically targeted vulnerable, elderly East Asians.

Now, my family is primarily of Irish descent, and people often like to remind me that the Irish were treated poorly, were excluded from jobs, back in the day. There are those startling images of the NO IRISH NEED APPLY signs from the late nineteenth century. There were political cartoons that depicted Irish people as apes and gorillas. There were even Ku Klux Klan posters attacking the Irish and Irish Catholicism in the 1920s, when my grandfather was growing up in his Irish immigrant household. That all happened too.

But unlike the fear, violence, and racism so many Asian

Americans face today, that kind of anti-Irish discrimination has long since vanished. So what changed for people of Irish descent? Why do they no longer face the discrimination and hate that people of Chinese (or any other Asian) descent still do today?

What's different for me is that in America I am much more *white* than I am Irish. I'm Irish American, sure, but I'm perceived to be white, and therefore I live white. And *that* makes all the difference.

For example, I lived in Queens, New York, for a number of years and had a neighbor down the hall who'd recently emigrated from Egypt. We were friendly, helping each other out by carrying packages up to each other's door, or I might lend him a hand fixing something in his computer and he might bring by a plate of some food he made. He'd told me many times about coming here from Egypt, but he didn't know much about my family history, and one day he asked where I was from. I jokingly said I was from Boston, but I knew what he was asking, and he clarified.

"No. Your blood. Where is your family from?"

I told him my family hailed mostly from Ireland.

"Oh, I thought you were German," he said. "Same thing."

At first I laughed. In my mind I understood a very large difference between German and Irish heritage, but his mistake didn't offend me at all. I had no stake in really caring if he thought I was Irish or German. In fact, I thought his line, "same thing," was funny. But as I further reflected on those words, I began to think about the impact of that assumption. In Queens those of us who were of German descent and those of us who were of Irish descent were very much the same thing: we were white. And by being white, when we walked into a corner store, when we walked into an office building, when we walked into a bank, when we walked into a school or an airport or anywhere in the United States, people rarely looked at us with suspicion, people rarely glanced at us and saw a stereotype instead of a person. In many cases people wouldn't even notice us at all unless we made ourselves known and spoke up about why we'd walked into the building in the first place.

I'd heard my neighbor talk about the difficulties he'd had with people looking at him condescendingly at the bank when he went in to apply for a loan. About how when he went to the public pool, some of the employees watched him, scrutinized him—as if they feared he might harm someone if they didn't keep their eye on him, when all he was doing was going for his morning swim.

But none of that had ever happened to me. Those are experiences I've never had when I've interacted with anyone in a position of authority. I've never been made to feel like I don't belong in a public pool or a bank or a school or any public institution. *Because I am white.*

Nowhere I go are people of authority *concerned* about my presence.

But look at this on the flip side. Motel 6 recently had to pay a huge $8.9 million lawsuit because some locations were regularly reporting guests with "Spanish surnames" to Immigration and Customs Enforcement. Think about that! Employees at Motel 6 simply looked at a guest's last name, saw something they assumed—they had to assume, how could they even know?—was a "Spanish" last name, and then reported that guest, in an effort to try to get them deported! No one was doing that to people with Irish or German (or British or Norwegian, etc.) last names!

So, again: What happened? How and why did only certain ethnic groups come to be *perceived* as "white"? As a "racial" identity, or category, known as "white"?

Well, first, ethnicity is something meaningful. For example, a person might be Kurdish or Igbo. Puerto Rican. Dominican. Catalan. Czech. Chinese or, even more specifically, Han, Zhuang, or Hui. These are cultural ethnicities. And, of course, people might have family that descends from different parts of the world and thus identify with a multiplicity of ethnicities. And celebrating one another's ethnicities and cultural customs and rituals and traditions is exciting! *That's* the beauty and breadth of ethnicity. That's the *reality*.

What's more is that someone might identify ethnically as Hispanic but identify racially as white . . . or not white. Official government forms in the United States allow for people who identify as Hispanic to also self-identify *racially* as they choose—because their Hispanic ethnicity is not a "race."

None of those ethnicities are "races." And any grouping of people from various regions of the world can't be placed in a neat category or a "race." Isn't a person whose Han family immigrated to Italy three generations earlier Italian? And what is "Italian," exactly? Italy's separate regions only unified in 1848, and it only became an actual country in 1946! The point is that ethnicity is complex, multifaceted, and very much a cultural reality.

This was true for Irish, German, Polish, Italian, and many other European immigrants in America in the late nineteenth and early twentieth centuries as well—they, like Chinese immigrants at the time, were seen as, and treated as, "racially other than" white (primarily Anglo-Saxon) Americans.

But within a relatively short period of time (and because of a complex intersection of political and economic influences) these European immigrants, and certainly their children, were seen (perceived or identified) less and less by their ethnic background and more and more as simply "white." Whiteness erased (at least to some extent) their Irish, German, Italian, Polish, or Greek heritage, but that erasure granted something else: being white, living as white people.

So long, Erin go bragh (that's Irish Gaelic, loosely translated as "Ireland forever") and hello, white privilege.

Now, there's absolutely something sad about that erasure (there really is, I truly believe that), but the white privilege I'm left with in return becomes my ticket into that other, privileged America divided by racism.

What's even more complicated about this whole "perceived to be white" business, however, is that it isn't tied to ethnicity, either. If someone who was Black, or Iranian, or any combination of cultural identities had climbed into the pickup with that Uber driver that morning, so long as that person was "perceived to be white" by the driver, was assumed to be "white like him," he would have spoken just as easily, freely, and conspiratorially to the passenger as he did to me, right?

Doesn't that make this whole "who is white?" question utterly confusing? Maybe even nonsensical?

Yeah, *but*, at the end of the day, even if I don't know what "white" means exactly, I still *know* I'm white. I'm a white boy for sure. That's how people know me. That's how people see me. It's how other people identify me.

When I check the boxes about my identity when I'm doing standardized tests or when I go to the doctor's office or when I'm filling out paperwork for the government or even when I click through some ad in my Instagram feed and I have to fill out a survey first about my demographics, I check the box for "white."

But does that even make sense? I'm white because I check a box for white on official forms? I'm white because people see me—perceive me—to be white?

It's how I'm identified. Not Black, not Latinx, Asian, or Pacific Islander, not Native American or Indigenous, not not not—I'm identified as white. White, with all its privileges. And yet had I ever heard anyone talking about white American identity?

Because . . . ahhhh! Just saying those words ("white American identity") feels weird. It really does.

And it's starting to seem like, culturally speaking, "being white" just means having racial privilege or advantage. But that still doesn't answer the question of who is white, does it?

Maybe that's because trying to figure out what white racial identity is *is* confusing, because, well, race itself is a little confusing. Frankly, "race" doesn't make any sense at all!

So maybe, before I can even start to talk about the "white" part of white racial identity, it'd help to know a little more about racial identity in general.

6

Chicken-and-Egg Problem . . . Solved!

You know why I find race a little confusing?

I'm just going to flat-out say it: *because it's totally bogus.*
That's right. It's a sham. An illusion. A fast one that's been
pulled over on all of us.

This is the truth: "race" has *no basis in biological fact.*
That's right! There is no scientific way to group people
into clear and distinct "races." And what's more? Get this:
all human beings across the entire planet share the same

99.9 percent of our DNA. Thank you, Human Genome Project!

But—and this is the real "but"—the problem is that it still plays an enormous role in our everyday reality. So even though it is not a biological fact, you could call it a "social fact." That social fact is absolutely undeniable. "Race" as we *experience it* (even though it doesn't exist, biologically speaking) plays an irrefutable role in our lives.

But, but, butbutbut—we've been hearing about "race" our whole lives, you might be countering. Yeah! You're right! You *have* been hearing about race all your life! And maybe now, more than ever, we've been hearing about how it impacts nearly everything in our lives. Heck, I've been saying that so far too! Heckity heck, I just said it in the previous paragraph!

Well, yes. This whole weird "hey, this isn't real in biological fact, but it is totally real in social fact" stance was a confusing mess for me too until I learned a pretty simple way of understanding it. A clear way to understand it.

You know the whole conundrum of the chicken and the egg? Which came first? You know, like, in order for there to be a chicken, there needs to be an egg the little chick pecks its way out of to then grow up into a chicken, right? But where did that first egg come from? From a chicken. But where did that first chicken come from? Wasn't it an egg? But where'd that egg come from?

Aaarrrrrgggggghhh!!

Well, in many ways racism in America is complicated like that. There are scholars and journalists and teachers and writers and tons and tons of people who have done and are doing research about it, who are discovering new ways to think about where racism came from, how it developed, and why it stays with us. And we need to keep studying the nuances of all this. Because it *is* complicated.

But to get some kind of handle on it all, I point you to how the writer Ta-Nehisi Coates boiled it down to one very clear and understandable line, kinda answering the chicken-and-egg version of race and racism:

Which came first, race or racism? "Race is the child of racism," Coates said.

And it really is that simple. Racism came first.

Why? Because race is . . . completely made up. It's a construct. Throughout history, people have used junk science, bogus theories, and crap logic to try to "define" race. Because if people believed in the concept of "race," people with social power (those in political office, judges, rich people, etc.) could use it as an excuse to maintain that social power by saying things like "That 'race' belongs in the lower class" or "This 'race' doesn't belong in the United States" or other nonsense things that have nothing to do with race and everything to do with which people stay in power and which have a harder time accessing it.

But, okay, maybe you already know all this and you know race is not biological. Honestly, I didn't know that when I was growing up. I just kind of assumed it was biological because I didn't know what else to think—because no one taught me otherwise.

But because race *isn't* biological, it makes strange things like this true:

- A person considered "Black" in the United States might be considered "white" in Brazil or "colored" in South Africa.

- In the United States people of Mexican birth or ancestry were categorized as "white" until the 1930 census, when "Mexican" was added as its own separate "race." In the nearly one hundred years since then, their status has changed back and forth several times between "Hispanic" and "white."

- Over the course of the twentieth century in the United States, the racial categorization for immigrants from the Indian subcontinent changed from "Hindu" to "white" to "Asian Indian" to "South Asian" as the number of legally recognized "races" in the country expanded and contracted and changed over time.

- In the early twentieth century in the United States, there was debate about whether or not people of Japanese descent were "white" until a court case (nothing to do with science, remember) decided that they were not because of (and, yes, this is a direct quote) "the common understanding of the white man." The common what?! Of *who??* In other words, *racism*!

- At one point or another in US history, people from Germany, Ireland, Italy, Spain, Poland, and Greece were not considered "white"—but they are now. In fact, many of them were considered their own separate "races," such as Celtic, Slavic, Iberic, and Hebrew, while "white" was reserved for only Anglo-Saxon Americans.

Now consider these two statements that are true based on actual science and genetics:

> - A study showed that two "white" scientists of European ancestry had more genetic variation between them than either of them had with a third scientist who was Asian— Korean, to be specific.
>
> - "Ethnic groups in Western Africa are more genetically similar to ethnic groups in Western Europe than to ethnic groups in Eastern Africa. Race is a genetic mirage."

Go ahead and read those two sentences again. They're a little tricky to follow, but they're scientifically true and debunk any notion that "race" is something biological.

Is your mind blown?

The list of evidence like this goes on and on and on.

So, at the end of the day, none of us can tell a person's "race" just by looking at them. It's one of the reasons questions like "What are you?" or "Where are you from?" are often so hurtful to many people of the Global Majority living in America, because the person asking the question (often, though not always, a white person) is really asking: *What is your racial or ethnic background?*

And the answer might be complicated or not fit neatly into this artificial box we've invented called "race." Or maybe the person who has been asked that kind of question many times before already knows from experience that the person asking the question has a whole set of assumptions lined up for whatever the answer might be. Because tucked within *that* question is one of those needlelike stabs that dig deeper and sting sharper every time the question comes up, because it suggests they somehow look "less American"—which is so, SO, *SO* wrong.

> **Person 1:** "What are you?"
>
> **Person 2:** "I'm multiracial. My mother is Black and Japanese, and my father is Polish."
>
> **Person 1:** "Oh, that's funny. I thought you were from Brazil or something."
>
> **Person 2:** (Just blinks and tries not to look angry or sad or exhausted.)

No, Person 1. Please, no! That's actually *not funny* at all. Person 2 might be feeling any or all of the emotions behind those eyeblinks. Besides, why does Person 1 need to know Person 2's racial or ethnic background before Person 2 has decided to share it in the first place? Does Person 1 work for the US Census Bureau? Is it some kind of game? *Let's see if I can guess that person's racial identity!* How exactly is that "funny"?

All too often it's different for white people, especially when it's white people asking one another where they're from, because it's generally assumed they're already "from" the United States, and therefore the question actually implies, "Which state?" or "Which city?" Meaning: "Where in America?" not "Where outside America?" The only really weird or difficult thing about "being white" is that the definition of who is white in America has changed over time. Meaning, again, that "white" did not apply to some people in America at first—people who, like Italians, Germans, Irish, Poles, and others, are now included in the group called "white."

Yup. You got it. As I said, this really is a little strange and confusing . . . *because the whole concept of "race" is racist to begin with.*

Totally made up. To justify racism. And in America that has meant to uplift, advantage, privilege, and protect people who are considered "white."

Why don't more people know about how racism has shaped and defined "race" and, for white people, their "whiteness" in particular? Or talk about it?

Good question. Maybe this'll help explain *that.*

You know how when someone does a terrible thing, like, say, steals video game magazines from a store, and then they make up a lie to cover it up and that lie becomes a story, and they tell that story so many times that they might even believe it after a while?

That's how the story of "race" worked too.

But wait. Steal video game magazines? Why use that as an example?

So, quick story. (Oh, yes. You're right. I have way too many of these kinds of stories. And I'm going to tell them anyway.)

That same fool pocketing bottles of Strawberry Nesquik? Well, that guy, that fool—um, me—also stole magazines from a store, so he could try to impress his friends by having all these tips and tricks to beat the video games they all played.

Yeah, so, first, there were (way back when) stores that sold magazines that were about video games, and those magazines literally gave away the answers to beating some of the harder levels of some of the games. (Uh, yes, you're absolutely right—I was trying to impress people *by cheating*. Real cool.)

But when my friends figured out that I was able to beat the games only because I had these magazines, I realized how terrible that seemed, so I MADE UP A STORY ABOUT HOW I GOT THE MAGAZINES.

I told everyone they fell off the back of a delivery truck, and when I saw what they were, I realized I could really use them. But it wasn't my fault! They fell off the back of a truck! What was I supposed to do? Not use them?

Now (a) that's a ridiculous (not to mention hard-to-believe) lie, but my friends seemed to buy it at first, so I kept repeating it. Even a couple friends who were skeptical eventually stopped asking me about it, and even if they didn't believe me, they just stopped challenging me and let it slide.

But also (b): I. Was. Lying! Why was I doing this?

Well, one day I was sitting on my front steps with a few friends, telling them the story about the truck again, and my father happened to be standing at the front door. It was warm out, so the front door was open and he could hear everything I was saying through the screen door. Yup. He listened to me tell my story—who am I kidding, *my super ridiculous lie*—and when I was done, he came busting out the door, down the steps.

"BRENDAN MICHAEL KIELY!" he boomed. (You know when a parent throws in the middle name that you are absolutely f---ed. And I was.)

He hollered and yelled until I broke down, right there in front of my friends, and told him the truth. I told him I'd stolen the magazines from the store. I felt so miserably stupid. I'd been telling the lie for so long, I'd almost gotten to the point of believing it—that the magazines just fell in my lap. If you become too good at lying to yourself, you *become a lie* yourself. My lie, my con, was actually deeply hurting me.

And who wants to *be a lie?*

Well . . . actually. You know where this is going. Yup. It's all coming back to "race."

But first, I want to tell you one last thing about the magazines. My father marched me back into the store where I'd stolen them. He made me apologize to the owner. And we paid for them—or, you might say, my dad bailed me out of my debt. *And* it was only after having to apologize, after having to look the storeowner in the eye and tell him what I did, that I felt sick and tired of the person I'd been that year, stealing from two different corner stores.

I had to ask myself: Who had I been? And also, who did I want to be?

One thing I knew. I didn't want to lie like that anymore. I didn't want to live a lie. I didn't want to be a lie . . . which really does bring me back to "race."

Because "race" is a lie. "Being white" is a lie. There's no

such thing as a white person. As race. As whiteness. They are totally made up. They're constructs. But these false constructs—these lies—have been told so well and so frequently that too many of us believe them—and we basically don't even realize that what we assume is "the way things are" isn't actually *true*. It's all a con game!

In other words, again, race is not a biological fact—but it is a social fact. And what that looks like in reality is . . . well . . . racism.

And, as I mentioned, racism affects everything in our lives. Our education. Our housing. The food available to us. It affects our jobs and how much money we make. Our right to vote, how we vote, and whether or not people try to deny us that right to vote.

When I was growing up, I was taught that racism *denies*. It denies people their voting rights, their access to more valuable housing, their ability to compete for higher-paying jobs. The list of things racism denied was long—it *is* long.

But I never looked at it the other way around—I was never taught to look at it like this: if racism *dis*advantages some people, then it also *advantages* others. Think about it:

If one person is *denied* more valuable housing, another person *gets* it.

If one person is denied a higher-paying job, someone *else* gets it.

And if you deny one person something, you're giving the *advantage* to another person. Or *privileges*, right? And with racism, the denials give those advantages to—you guessed it—

white people. So the privileges go to white people . . . and we are right back to *white privilege*.

White people have given themselves a leg up at the cost of holding others down. Those "legs up" are white privileges—the privileges go to white people! So to *have* white privilege, there has to be racism.

Which means: white privilege, in and of itself, is racism.

Whoa.

Yup.

That's a lot to take in.

I know.

But hold up a second.

Does this mean that all the horrors and injustices of racism are my fault and your fault, if you are white like me? Should all white people sit here with our chins tucked to our chests? No. No! Have hope! That's the whole *reason* for the need to talk about this *now*. If we see what *has been*, we can make changes to *do better* than our past. First we need to know, truly understand, how things got so bad and why they stay so bad. If we don't know, we can't change. And if we *do* know, we have no excuse not to do better. And doing better is better—for *everyone*.

7

Cheating to Win

So my birthday is July 2. Yup. I'm just throwing that out there. And when I was growing up, it was always kind of a bummer that I didn't get to have a party in class like all the other kids did whose birthdays fell sometime between September and June. But I convinced myself it was cool that I basically got to celebrate my birthday on the country's birthday every year. All right, I know what you're thinking: I'm two days off. But, nope—July 2 is actually the date when the Continental Congress voted for independence; John Adams even wrote about how July 2 would be the day Americans celebrated their nation's birthday with fireworks. So even though fireworks crashed and splashed over Boston two days later—the wrong day!—every year, I still kinda pretended a few of those glittering showers in the sky were for me.

Sure, it was a bit of a con game I played to make myself feel better, but there was another con game happening on July 2 . . . in 1776. You might remember these famous lines from the Declaration of Independence (that were later dated, yes, July 4, on the document—but whatever):

> We hold these truths to be self-evident,
> that all men are created equal, that they
> are endowed by their Creator with certain
> unalienable Rights, that among these are
> Life, Liberty, and the pursuit of Happiness.

The thing is, these words were a con game. How? Because they had to do with whiteness. With who was white. Or, rather, who wasn't. Because even though these lofty lines said "all men," the people writing it didn't actually mean *all* men. And what the @#&%? about the women?! (Well, the talk about sexism and misogyny is a whole *other* talk this white boy will definitely have with his son—but the focus of *this* talk is about race, so . . . back to it.)

Those lofty lines about "Life, Liberty, and the pursuit of Happiness" applied only to white people. That was mostly implied at first, but later, in 1790, the Naturalization Act nailed it down in very specific writing by granting US citizenship to only "white persons" of "good character." And that racial distinction was not eliminated entirely until 1952.

In fact, the Naturalization Act's racializing of immigration policy was only one piece in a complicated puzzle that created a legal and socially enforced set of rules, "norms," customs, and laws that laid the foundation for, and continue to shape, a society-wide system that supports and prioritizes white privilege.

Want a little (or a lot of) proof? Take a look:

TIME LINE OF POLICIES, SOCIAL CUSTOMS, AND LAWS THAT INSTITUTIONALIZED AND SYSTEMIZED WHITE PRIVILEGE IN THE UNITED STATES

time	what it is	what it did
1500s and onward	Perpetual war against Indigenous people	Created an "us and them" ("colonists" vs. Indigenous people) distinction
1619	Arrival of first slave ship carrying more than twenty human beings who became the first enslaved people in the English colonies that eventually became the United States of America	Created a second "us and them" demarcation: people with rights and people without them
1676	Bacon's Rebellion	Created a legal distinction and separation among Indigenous people, enslaved people, and poor "white" people to disrupt those three groups from working together to overthrow rich "white" people
1787	Three-Fifths Compromise	Brokered a deal that legally constituted enslaved human beings to count as only three fifths of a human being in order to influence the number of representatives allotted to a state in which slavery was legal and affect that state's federal taxes

1790	Naturalization Act	Designated citizenship for only "white persons" of "good character"
1830	Indian Removal Act	US Army forcibly relocated Cherokees, Creeks, and other eastern Indigenous tribes to west of the Mississippi, which provided white families the opportunity to own the land instead and buoyed inherited generational wealth for white families in America
1862	Homestead Act	Further forcibly removed Indigenous people from their homelands and "opened" more than 270 million acres (more than 10 percent of the total land area of the United States) for wealth building; 1.6 million white families were granted land (for free!) and the opportunity to accrue wealth
1877	First "Jim Crow" laws	Legal system of segregation that elevated economic opportunity and civil rights of white people over Black people in particular; the laws effectively dismantled new laws and customs of the Reconstruction, which attempted to address some kind of racial justice after the Civil War and the end of slavery, reimposing legalized racial injustice
1882	Chinese Exclusion Act	Banned immigration from China and other Asian countries to minimize population growth of people from East Asia in the United States; the act simultaneously granted immigration rights to people from European countries, effectively increasing what was and became the "white" population in the United States

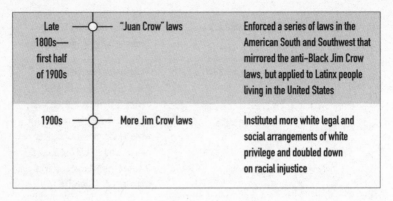

Late 1800s—first half of 1900s	"Juan Crow" laws	Enforced a series of laws in the American South and Southwest that mirrored the anti–Black Jim Crow laws, but applied to Latinx people living in the United States
1900s	More Jim Crow laws	Instituted more white legal and social arrangements of white privilege and doubled down on racial injustice

This is another list that goes on and on and on. Bet you noticed a pattern here—I thought you would!

In every case, whether through violence, social custom, or law, white people, and most often white men, were given advantages over everyone else. In other words, using those levers (violence, social custom, and law), white privilege was *systematized* into our way of life here in the USA.

And once those systems were in place, they branched out and affected so many other aspects of life. Schooling. Club memberships. Landownership opportunities. Even who was or wasn't allowed to have a public library card.

Although policies were sometimes put in place to try to correct the injustices of this systematized white privilege, all too often those efforts were quickly dismantled. For example, after the Civil War, during the period of our history referred to as the Reconstruction (the mid-1860s to the late 1870s), many policies were put in place that created new opportunities for Black people that had previously been denied to them. One of those opportunities was employment in the federal government. Not only were federal jobs now available, there was no segregation in those government offices.

Black people and white people worked right alongside each other until 1913, when Woodrow Wilson's administration ended this by instituting racial segregation in government agencies: putting up dividers, creating different office spaces, even, in one case—when the Black employee's work required him to be in the midst of his white colleague's office space—constructing a cage around the Black employee's workspace!

In fact, many of President Wilson's policies worked to reinstitute and reinforce pre-Reconstruction racial hierarchies and divisions, even going so far that, after the segregation had been firmly established, many of the jobs held by Black employees were deemed "unnecessary" and quickly dissolved—effectively wiping out the job opportunities that had become available during Reconstruction.

So the people (men) who sat down to write that famous line—"Life, Liberty, and the pursuit of Happiness"—were talking out of both sides of their mouths. And too many of the people in charge of building and evolving our democracy worked to segregate and *racialize* that democracy (remember the "two Americas"?). Because all too many of the policies, social customs, and legal documents that followed those first founding documents of our nation made a clear distinction between which people those initial high ideals of our democracy applied to—white people—and which they didn't.

I mean, just looking through the abbreviated time line above, it's pretty clear how, as a nation, the people in power sat down and *legalized, institutionalized,* and *systematized* racism in America.

So maybe you're asking, *Why'd they do that?*

Well, in the beginning it was so that some people could, on the one hand, build a new country based on "natural rights" (Life, Liberty, and the pursuit of Happiness) while, on the other hand, justify the displacement of Indigenous people and the constant warfare and genocide against them, as well as the loathsome and dehumanizing institution of slavery. How else could a people claim, for instance, that everybody had the right to "Liberty" in this country when some people were *enslaved*—the very opposite of liberty? And if a person is driven from their homeland and their way of life, where are their rights to "Life"?

It was all done so that certain rights would be granted only to people of a certain "race" and the people of that "race" would get the advantages of those rights. And this continued from the founding documents on, throughout American history, as the time line on pp. 64–66 shows. So *if* a person was considered "white" in the United States, *being white* came with those advantages, privileges, over other people in the United States.

So white privilege *is* the cheat?
Yup.
And that was the plan?
Yup. It was literally designed that way.

No way, you're thinking. *You make it sound like a conspiracy,* you're thinking.

Well, that's because it *was* one—a conspiracy to put white people (and white men in particular) at the top of the food chain, again and again and again, by writing white privilege into laws and social customs, again and again and again.

That plan, that design, that system created by that continuation of law after law and social code after social code led to what *systemic white privilege* looks like today:

- **Ten richest Americans (seven of whom are among the ten richest in the world):** 100 percent white
- **US Congress:** 90 percent white
- **US governors:** 96 percent white
- **Top military advisors:** nearly 100 percent white
- **People who decide which TV shows we see:** 93 percent white
- **People who decide which books we read:** 90 percent white
- **People who decide which news is covered:** 85 percent white
- **People who decide which music is produced:** 95 percent white
- **People who directed the one hundred top-grossing films of all time worldwide:** 95 percent white
- **Teachers:** 82 percent white
- **Full-time college professors:** 84 percent white

And keep in mind: white people are only 60.1 percent of the total US population today! In fact, as of 2019, white people are only 49.9 percent of Americans aged sixteen or younger. So these figures showing the percentages of white people in prominent positions of power in America are kind of astounding, aren't they?

How History Lives in the Present

Often white people in positions of power tell stories about how they (or their parents or grandparents) "pulled themselves up by their bootstraps." And, yes, people work hard. For those who do, there are often financial rewards that one generation can pass down to the next to assist them in their own pursuit of "Life, Liberty, and . . . Happiness." But if the previous generations in your family were white, "hard work" is not the whole story.

My Irish immigrant family worked hard in the 1920s

and '30s. But they also can't claim to have achieved everything they achieved solely with "their own two hands," if, for example, my grandfather had access to the benefits of the GI Bill after he served in World War II. Benefits that enabled him to go to college and get a loan for his first house, both of which provided him and my grandmother the opportunity to lay a foundation of financial support for their quickly growing family—benefits most Black, Indigenous, Latinx (particularly Mexican American), and Japanese American soldiers (who, like Black soldiers, were segregated within the armed services) were excluded from accessing when they returned from war. Even Chinese American soldiers who could, and often did, enlist as "white" later faced discrimination back home and were likewise excluded from accessing these benefits.

Here are the whopping results of benefits provided by the 1944 GI Bill:

- Nearly nine million veterans received close to $4 billion from the bill's unemployment compensation program.

- 49 percent of college admissions in 1947 were veterans.

- The home loans afforded veterans under the bill allowed them to move into newly built neighborhoods and towns (the suburbs, basically), which quickly became more valuable than a lot of the property in crowded cities or on remote farmlands.

And who got these benefits? Nearly all of them went to white veterans like my grandfather. That doesn't take away from all the hard work my grandfather (or many other white veterans) put into his education and career and family. It doesn't take away from the setbacks and the pain he also felt along the way. It doesn't take away from the political and social jockeying he had to manage to make his way up the corporate ladder. But the GI Bill gave him a huge advantage over other veterans who were not white. Gave him opportunities fellow American veterans of the Global Majority weren't able to partake in at all.

Case in point:

COLLEGE TUITION AND COST OF LIVING STIPENDS

For my white grandfather:

- My grandpa made use of the benefit to earn an MS in chemistry and pursue further job-opportunity-enhancing education in statistical quality control.
- Because he got a college degree and an advanced degree in a specialized field, he had access to a higher-paying job.
- Once he started in the field of plastics, he could pursue other, more lucrative job possibilities only available to people who had first received the education, then worked in that specialized field.
- He climbed the corporate ladder and found even more lucrative pay in management.
- This allowed him to help build wealth for his family.

For American veterans of the Global Majority:

- Many Black, Indigenous, and Latinx veterans could not get access to the education stipends or were steered by Veterans Administration officials away from pursuing college toward menial and physical labor positions.
- Even those who pursued college often found admission difficult because of racist and exclusionary admissions policies.

- Without a college degree or study in a specialized field, many Black, Indigenous, and Latinx veterans, in particular, were forced to take low-wage jobs.
- Many of the low-wage jobs offered no means of further professional advancement and therefore no substantial pay increases.
- This in turn made it very difficult for these veterans to build wealth for their families.

UNEMPLOYMENT AND HEALTHCARE BENEFITS

For my white grandfather:

- Most benefits were administered by the nearly all-white Veterans Administration at a time when racial discrimination was high.
- He didn't pursue the unemployment benefit, and he had alternative access to healthcare.

For American veterans of the Global Majority:

- Because most benefits were managed by nearly all-white administrations, personal bias made accessing both the unemployment and the healthcare benefits difficult.
- With healthcare not as accessible, it was even harder for out-of-work Black, Indigenous, and Latinx veterans to find employment.

HOME LOAN BENEFITS

For my white grandfather:

- With the home loan opportunities available to them, my grandparents were able to buy a first home in rapidly growing Binghamton, New York.
- That first home gained value quickly, so as my grandpa's family grew, he had more opportunity and access to "upgrade": buy one house, sell it for a profit, use the money gained to buy a more valuable house that gained yet more value while the family lived in it, sell that house for a profit, and then start the cycle all over again.
- These early homeowning opportunities provided my grandparents with the financial foundation to support their quickly growing family.

For American veterans of the Global Majority:

- Because of racist administrators, bank employees, and policies, many Black, Indigenous, and Latinx veterans could not access the same home loan opportunities that white veterans could and therefore could not own homes of the same value.

- Even if they did have the money, the banks, real estate brokers, and community leaders in those quickly valuing suburbs effectively created segregated, mostly "whites-only" communities.
- Thus opportunities to accrue substantial family wealth through real estate and home-ownership were denied to most Black, Indigenous, and Latinx veterans.

Now, I loved my grandfather when he was alive. I still love him. I love my grandmother, and I love my whole family. (Hey, fam, I really do love you all!) But it is also okay to be honest and say that my grandfather had access to a "head start" and a financial springboard just not available to most Black and Indigenous veterans in particular.

And it is just as honest to say that people like me, two generations removed from the opportunity my grandfather had access to, have benefited from that access in a way that grandchildren of Black and Indigenous World War II veterans have not.

So, all right. There were all these cheats put in place way back when, and now some people—people who are white—reap the advantages (privileges) of those cheats. And it's easy to assume (I mean, many of us so often *do* assume) that that was the past and that there were more racists in the past, and therefore the systemic problems we are left with today that perpetuate white privilege are *solely* the ripple effects of those long-ago discriminatory actions.

And while, yes, that is partly true—the ripple effects of those actions from the past are most certainly still making waves today—that's not the whole story.

The whole story includes the fact that there are *still* people out there today rigging the system to disadvantage people who are not white.

Look at voting, for instance.

In the state of Florida in the 2000 presidential election:

- Fifty-eight thousand "alleged felons" were purged from voter eligibility. Black people were only 11 percent of the registered voters, but they were 44 percent of the people purged from voter eligibility.

- In some of the counties with the highest percentage of Black voters, Black people were ten times more likely than white people to have their votes not count due to some kind of "voting error."

- Across the whole state, 179,855 ballots were invalidated by Florida election officials; the race between Al Gore and George Bush was ultimately won by only 537 votes that year.

- Though Black voters were overwhelmingly more supportive of Al Gore, George Bush won that state and, by winning that state, won the presidency.

In the state of Wisconsin in the 2016 presidential election:

- The state's voter ID law targeted primarily Black people, Indigenous people, and many people of the Global Majority, in general.

- This law alone suppressed two hundred thousand votes.

- Donald Trump won the state by only 22,748 votes.

In the state of Georgia in the 2018 gubernatorial election:

- Brian Kemp, a white man, who was Georgia's secretary of state (and therefore in charge of elections), erased more than 560,000 people's voter eligibility in a single day in July 2017. They were people who had been marked for not having voted in enough recent elections and therefore had "lost their right to vote"—what's called a "use-it-or-lose-it scheme." Kemp then announced he was running for governor in the 2018 election. But he remained secretary of state the entire time, so he was the officer in charge of his own election! That's like being the quarterback *and* the referee of the game! (But that doesn't seem to be illegal because it's a system that somehow allows for that kind of thing to be okay.)

- Commissions found proof that at least 340,000 voter registrations had been purged incorrectly. They also found that Kemp (as voter referee of his own election) blocked the registration of at least fifty thousand would-be voters, 80 percent of whom were Black, Latinx, and Asian.

- Kemp won the election for governor, beating Stacey Abrams, a Black woman, by only roughly fifty-five thousand votes.

Where I come from, that's called cheating.

And who did this cheating *disadvantage*? Voters who are not white.

And who did this cheating then *advantage*? Voters who are white.

This isn't political commentary; it's simply telling the truth. When it came to voting in each of these instances, white people's votes were privileged (in other words, counted!) when many people of the Global Majority's votes were not, particularly Black people's votes. And that privilege decided the results of those major elections. If *everyone's* votes had been counted, we would have had different people in office, which would have meant different people in power, which would have meant different current laws and political appointees in place.

It would be an entirely different America right now.

Think about that.

So, just a repeat for those of us snoozing in the back row: It's all about racism. Racism to give white people advantages,

advantages that started "back then" but that still have impact today, still exist today.

And what's wild—except, not really; really, it's kind of sadly understandable—is that you can see that history living right here in our present today. I mean, it's like one of those double-exposure photographs, where it looks like there's this ghost of an image hovering over another image.

Like this:

Do you see the young woman there? That's our present.

Do you see the skeletal fibers of a leaf? That's our history . . . living in us, living on us, living with us.

There are many examples of how our history lives in our present, just like a double-exposed photograph.

For example:

Back in the late 1800s companies like Southern Pacific Railroad sent agents to Mexico in search of "cheap labor" and encouraged people to immigrate to the United States for those jobs, even if they had to come into the country illegally.

Fast-forward forty years to the 1920s and '30s: violence and resentment among white Americans against the immigrants had grown so much that the government responded, not to protect the dignity and safety of Mexican Americans and people of Latin American descent, but rather in support of the white people. In Los Angeles, for instance, Olvera Street was a thriving marketplace and community gathering spot for the Mexican and Latinx American communities. Then, in a terrifying raid in 1931, police rounded up over four hundred Mexicans and Mexican Americans and deported them to Mexico, *regardless of whether or not they were American citizens*.

This was only one incident among so many in which white Americans resented Mexicans and the Latinx community in the United States and law enforcement officials supported those white resentments through brutal and discriminatory deportation raids. In fact, during the 1920s and '30s the US government forcibly removed and deported nearly *two million* people of Mexican descent—60 percent of whom were American citizens!

And like that double-exposed image we just looked at, that past seeps into our present.

Some more examples:

Then	Now
The California Land Act of 1851 effectively created a new and nearly impossible hurdle for Mexican Americans (only recently "made" American after 55 percent of Mexico became part of the United States after the Mexican–American War) to prove they "owned" land their families had been living on for generations. This enabled white squatters (and especially prospectors during the gold rush) to then lay "claim" to the land and legally boot Mexican Americans off it.	In 2018 in Iowa City, Iowa, Latinx people were denied home loans four times more often than white people were.
The 1855 California Anti-Vagrancy Act targeted anyone who looked of "Spanish and Indian blood," who could be thrown in jail for any number of "disorderly" reasons and then punished and made to work "hard labor"—i.e., prison labor (a form of state-run slavery).	In 2003 the clothing company Abercrombie & Fitch was accused of refusing to hire people of color, in particular a great number of Latinx people, because they did not look like the "all-American models" in their ads—who were white.
In the 1840s white American government officials, newspapers, and other influential voices used the phrase "Manifest Destiny" to justify the genocide of Native American people, cultures, and ways of life, as well as to justify American expansion across the North American continent (overtaking 55 percent of what was once Mexico) and colonial dominion and subjugation over Central and South American countries (and likewise the people from those countries) in the time since.	"You'd be surprised!" President Ronald Reagan said in 1982, after his first official trip to Central America. "They're all individual countries!"

Then and now, those anti-Mexican, anti-Indigenous, anti–Central American, and anti–South American sentiments, ideas, policies, and social customs all worked to give huge advantage to . . . white people. Then and now, the whole system's been rigged to privilege white people.

Now, did *you* write the unfair policy undergirding the California Land Act? No, of course not. You weren't even around then. In fact, it's possible your whole family wasn't even in the United States yet, like most of mine wasn't. However, that doesn't give you a "get-out-of-white-privilege-free card." Because if we are white in America today, we live with the privileges that history built and passed down to us in the present.

The thing is, there are ways out of this mess. Ways to break down the rigged system. People (especially many Black and Indigenous people, and other people of the Global Majority in the United States) have been working hard to bust it up and break it down.

And the good news is, we can—and must—be a part of this. And by "we," I mean people out there who are white like me. We can be a part of seeking justice for all.

But first? We need to understand more about what we're up against.

So, all right. If our cheating-to-win history led to a rigged system in our present, you might be asking, *What does that system look like?*

Well, that's a good question. Because knowing what it looks like, what it is, will help us see *how we can be a part of seeking justice for all.*

9

The Entire System
Is Rigged

So, you getting hungry, by chance?

Let's talk about school lunch.

I mean, best part of the school day, right?

Well, imagine it's lunchtime, and you're staaarving, and then you're told that half your class can't have lunch today. Are being *denied* lunch. No pizza. No ice-cream-scoop plop of potato mush. No carton of milk. Not even that little cell-phone-sized bottle of water. If you're one of those kids, not only would you be pretty bummed, but your entire school day after lunch would be much harder than if you're one of the kids who gets to have lunch. You'd be hungry.

You'd be angry.

You'd be hangry—I mean, I get *hangry* whenever I miss a meal.

You'd also have a harder time paying attention. Let's say geometry class follows lunch. (Little bit of trivia: I nearly failed geometry all four quarters of my sophomore year—just squeaked by enough to pass.) Anyway, geometry is always after lunch, and it requires the whole class paying attention to the teacher as she solves problems on the board at the front of the classroom. Day after day the kids who get lunch would pretty much be able to pay better attention than you could, because remember, you're hangry. *Totally* not fair! You'd probably look around that room and say to yourself, *Those kids have an advantage over me.* They have lunch privileges you don't have. *Why do they get to eat lunch and I don't?*

And the "get-lunch kids" wouldn't even notice. They'd just see it as *living*. While *you'd* see their living as having advantages. You'd work as hard as they do, but they'd get lunch and you wouldn't.

I'd bet that, eventually, you'd be very, very pissed off about that.

So I'm betting that you'll probably feel the same way about *this*:

For close to eighteen million children in the United States, going to school hungry is an *everyday* reality. In fact, if every classroom in America mirrored the national average, that would mean nearly 25 percent of *your* class-mates (one in four students in your class) are going hungry *right now*.

They might not get breakfast. Or lunch. Or dinner. Or some combination of the three. They might be sitting in front of you. Behind you.

Or you might be the one who knows this all too well.

This is called "food insecurity." Food insecurity is a thing, and how it breaks down by race is an even bigger thing. I'm sure you can see where this is going:

- About 16.5 percent of US households with children experience food insecurity for their children (an estimated 13.9 million children). Thirteen million kids in America are hungry, on a daily basis. That is a horrifying reality for far too many families. But when you look at the information by race, the statistics are even more alarming.

- About 30 percent of all Black households in the United States with children experience food insecurity for their children.

- About 25 percent of all Latinx households in the United States with children experience food insecurity for their children.

- Less than 10 percent of all white households in the United States with children experience food insecurity for their children.

Don't get me wrong—for any household struggling to feed their kids, hunger is terrible and real. But it is also a fact that child food insecurity affects Black and Latinx families far worse than white families.

You can even say that white families, as a group, are food *privileged*, because they have greater food security for their children.

And guess what? Students who have regular access to food score 17.5 percent higher on standardized math exams. That difference could make or break passing a class. (Remember me saying I barely passed geometry? I definitely would have failed if I'd been hungry all year.) And if food access can make or break passing a class, it can make or break graduating from high school or getting into your college of choice.

Is that fair? Of course not!

Is that right? Of course not!

But is it reality? Unfortunately, yes.

You may not have given this a lot of thought (or you might have had to), but a lot goes into feeding a young person. You have to think about the *system* behind it: How much money does a family make? Where do they live? What kind of food is available near where they live? Do they have time to shop easily or not? Does someone have time to cook the food? That's just a handful of questions we could ask about the system needed to keep kids fed. They all impact how a family is able (or not able) to feed their children.

And because a higher percentage of the families who are food privileged are white—dramatically more so than

Black or Latinx families—it's racial injustice. In other words, racism.

And because food privilege and food insecurity are part of a *system*, we can call it "systemic racism."

Food insecurity isn't the only example of racial injustice in a system in our country. Here are a few others, but only a few. Because there are just too many.

In the system/institution of incarceration (jail):

- Research shows that white people and Black people use and sell drugs at the same rate.

- However, Black people are five times more likely to go to prison for drug possession and twelve times more likely to be wrongly convicted of all drug crimes (possession and intent to sell) than white people.

- One in every 106 white men in America is in prison; one in every 36 Latinx men; one in every 15 Black men.

In the system/institution of education:

- Despite the fact that racial segregation in public schools has been illegal since 1954, as of 2019, more than half the country's schoolchildren are in racially segregated schools that are either more than 75 percent white or more than 75 percent nonwhite.

- Those predominantly white public K–12 schools receive $23 billion more in funding than their predominantly nonwhite counterparts.

- 25 percent of schools with the highest percentage of Black and Latinx students do not offer Algebra II; 33 percent do not offer chemistry.

- Black students are more than three times as likely as white students to attend a school where less than 60 percent of the teachers meet the state certification requirements. Latinx students are twice as likely to attend similar schools.

In the system/institution of business:

- White applicants receive 39 percent more callbacks on job applications than Black applicants with similar job qualifications.

- Job loss related to the COVID-19 pandemic has overwhelmingly disproportionately affected Latinx, Black, and Asian workers.

In the system/institution of healthcare:

- Although approximately 14 percent of US residents do not have health insurance, 25 percent of all Latinx people in the United States do not have health insurance.

- 20 percent of Latinx people report experiencing discrimination in healthcare situations. And 17 percent of Latinx people report avoiding healthcare situations to avoid encounters of discrimination.

- Black people are more than 3.5 times more likely to die of COVID-19 than white people. Latinx people are nearly two times more likely to die of COVID-19 than white people.

In the system/institution of housing:

- Black and Latinx people face housing discrimination an estimated four million times a year.

- 17 percent of Native Americans, 25 percent of Asian Americans, 31 percent of Latinx Americans, and 45 percent of Black Americans report facing discrimination when trying to rent or buy a home.

- Homes in Black neighborhoods have been undervalued by an average of $48,000 due to racial bias, resulting in $156 billion in cumulative losses across the country.

- In the 2007 housing crash Black families were twice as likely to enter foreclosure (essentially lose their homes and go bankrupt) than white families.

- Fifty-eight out of every one thousand Native American households lack plumbing, compared to three out of every one thousand white households.

Again, these are just a few examples. We could kick up statistics in essentially any system/institution in America and you'd see the same types of results. This is what people are talking about when they talk about "systemic" (or "structural" or "institutional") racism. And almost always the ones who benefit, who gain from it, are white.

In other words, it's white privilege.

Some people say they don't believe in white privilege. But it isn't a question of who believes what. White privilege is simply being a white person in America. If you are white in America, you are privileged in your relationship to most social systems and institutions in America.

Another way to think about how this racism/white privilege can be systemic is to look at how some of those systems or institutions intersect and how those intersections affect people's lives.

For example, look at some of the intersecting policies during President Bill Clinton's administration in the 1990s. There's a whole lot of background to this, but to keep things a little simpler and clearer, it helps to know that by around 1990 many Democrats were sick of losing votes and political power to Republicans who were calling them "soft on crime." In his run for president and during his presidency Clinton declared, "No one can say I am soft on crime," and he set out to prove that in the policies he advocated for and supported.

And here's what happened:

"The Clinton administration's 'tough on crime' policies

resulted in the largest increases in federal and state prison inmates of any president in American history."

Look on p. 87 to remember who is most likely to have been among those prison inmates.

But that's only part of the story. Because in order to continue to show "toughness," the Clinton administration went on to "get tough" on welfare and critical family support programs: The president endorsed and signed the Personal Responsibility and Work Opportunity Reconciliation Act, which, among many other things, cut (for a person's lifetime!) eligibility for welfare and food stamps for anyone convicted of a drug felony—even only a onetime possession of marijuana.

Again, look back to p. 87 to see who is most likely to get searched, who is most likely to get caught with, and who is most likely to get charged with possession of drugs. Furthermore, look back to see who is most likely to receive a callback for a job interview—and therefore more likely to get a job and less likely to need the help of welfare and food stamps.

And it doesn't stop there!

In a continued effort to show "toughness," Clinton implemented the "One Strike and You're Out" Initiative for federal housing programs, a policy that made anyone convicted of a drug crime no longer eligible for federal housing and federal housing assistance—a policy that pushed thousands of people and families into homelessness.

So, again, if you look back to p. 89 to remember who has historically been most likely to be denied housing loans and discriminated against in pursuit of homeownership, and therefore more reliant on federal housing assistance, you can see the devastating pattern here.

Because the systems or institutions of incarceration, business, and housing have all disproportionately disadvantaged and harmed people of the Global Majority—in particular, Black people—this *interconnected systemic racism* has had a crushing effect on the families and communities caught between that threefold attack.

So why did the Clinton administration implement those "tough" policies while he was in office?

Clinton (and many other "New Democrats") wanted to show that the government was tough on "them" (remember the Uber driver's conspiratorial "you know what I mean"?) in order to inspire and get *white swing voters*. All that policy that enormously and disproportionately affected people of the Global Majority, and Black families and communities in particular, was part of a strategy to *appeal to white people*.

But maybe you're not one of those white people those policies were trying to entice? Maybe you're like, *Wow, I don't at all like how those kinds of policies target and harm people of the Global Majority.* And so maybe you're wondering, *What does all this systemic racism have to do with white people like me?*

Well, let's go back to our school-day scenario. Back to that lunch half the class wasn't allowed to have.

Okay, lunch is now over. The pizza crust had the perfect amount of crunch (for those who had it). But now we're back in the classroom. And something's going down. A quarter of the kids in your class are being seriously picked on, joked about—and they weren't ever given textbooks, by the way. Now they have to take the same test as the kids who have textbooks (some of whom have tutors to boot).

You? You have a textbook. You end up getting an A on the test.

The kid sitting next to you, with no book? No A. Or B. A C? Maybe . . .

If I'm one of the kids with a textbook and a belly full of crunchy-crusted pizza, I'd feel pretty gross about this. Sure, some of the kids who got picked on and didn't have a textbook got an A too. But more of them didn't. Do you think you would have gotten an A without a textbook? If you had your guard up all day, wondering where the next joke or insult might come from, do you think you could still get an A? Under those circumstances, I definitely would NOT get an A.

So, here's the deal. I had a textbook, and I got an A. You had a textbook, and you got an A. The kid who sits behind you got an A too, even though she didn't get a textbook. We should all feel awesome! But we don't. Not really. Know why? Because it's not an equal playing field. It's like winning a football game because you have eleven players on the field and the other team has only seven. So I'm feeling sad and angry and embarrassed all at once, because even though we are all in the same class, we are not being treated equally.

If this makes you feel not so great either, it's probably because we—white people—haven't *earned* it. We tell ourselves we've earned what we have, but we haven't, not totally. What we've earned often comes at the expense of other people not being able to earn it as easily.

Because white people have had an unfair advantage: white living, white privilege.

The *system*, in other words, *is rigged* in the favor of white people.

And I'm back to feeling like I did when I used to go to the corner store to steal gamer magazines: like a thief.

But here's a thought: What if we did something about it?

Like, what if those of us with textbooks in geometry class looked around and started making a lot of noise about the unfairness of some students having textbooks when others do not? What if we started talking to the students without textbooks, asking them how they feel, listening to them, even if what they said about us was hard to hear? After we'd all talked about it honestly and aired it all out, what if we all sat down to make a plan to do something together to change things—like make a stink about it, like demand to ask questions about the textbook imbalance at the next faculty meeting? We could do it.

What else could we do?

That's really the question at the bottom of all this. Kinda where all this is going.

See, for those of us who are white, we can't escape being white and living with white privilege, right? I mean, we were "born white," so to speak. It wasn't a *choice*. But what we do with our whiteness *is* a choice. *How* we live with it, what we *choose to do*—especially since we *can* act toward more racial justice—*that* is who we are as individuals.

But it's not my fault! some of you might be thinking. *I didn't make this happen, so why do I have to do something about it? Isn't that someone else's responsibility?*

Well . . .

If you are white like me, even though we didn't start this whole racially unjust mess, the mess was designed to provide us *today* with an entire system (of systemic racism) rigged in our favor . . .

. . . meaning, you and I inherited stupidly unfair amounts of privilege . . .

. . . and if we don't help eradicate racial injustice, we're actually helping maintain it—in fact, we could even be helping it get worse . . .

. . . so we have to take some responsibility for the system that is rigged in our favor by working backward and trying to undo some of that unfair rigging.

That is something we can do. Yup. All of us.

We can take some responsibility. How many times have you heard some adult in your life yammering at you about that?

Well, I sure got yammered at about taking responsibility. Especially by my dad. Especially the time I got caught doing what my friends and I used to call "ninja runs."

Oh, yeah. We didn't just think we were ninjas—we actually *called* ourselves ninjas.

I *know*. Wrong in so many ways. Here goes.

10

Ninja Runs

The summer between seventh and eighth grades, my friends and I—all of us white—were obsessed with ninjas. Every video game we played involved ninjas flying through the air doing roundhouse kicks. Every movie we watched depicted one martial arts star after another with his heel thrust above his head, spearing the air toward another villain. Everything we did and said was about ninjas.

There was this little stone wall in the yard across the street—the perfect place to practice our ninja somersaults. We would run toward the wall, jump over it, and somersault across the lawn beyond it. Or we'd run across the street to the elementary school, fly toward the building's brick wall, hitting it feetfirst, and then jump back, as if we were doing these amazing feats of physical prowess.

Basically, we were doing nothing. We were jumping into walls. Still, our imaginations ran wild. We could wear ninja costumes! Our friend Chris's parents were almost never home, so when we spent the night at his house, we had total freedom. Total freedom to take our larger-than-life ninja fantasies to a much higher level: like "real" ninjas, we set out on elaborate nighttime "missions."

First, we put on black sneakers, black socks, black sweatpants, and black hooded sweatshirts. We'd pull a T-shirt over our head, tie the arms behind our head so we could just see through the neckhole and only our eyes were visible. Then we'd run around the neighborhood, thinking up little adventures. "Ninja runs," we called them. (Um, just a little heads-up—I'm going to come back to this whole *four white kids* dressing as "ninjas" thing.)

Off we'd go, into the night. At first we weren't all that clever—we did things that were pretty basic. You know, your good old-fashioned ding-dong ditch, because that's a thing you do in the suburbs, right? We'd ring a doorbell, then run away into the shadows as somebody came to the door. We'd giggle wildly as the person kept saying "Hello?" and looked around confused.

Then we started thinking up more interesting ideas.

We swapped potted flowers from the front of the house to the back of the house. We moved people's lawn furniture from the front or back patio up onto the roof of their garage.

Not in any old way, mind you, but in the exact same setup: same two chairs staring at each other with the same table placed between them. As if somebody would get up in the morning, crawl up onto the roof of their garage, and kick back with a glass of juice or something!

Then we had our wildest—and most intrusive—idea.

Everyone in our neighborhood—probably nearly everyone in our town, in fact—who had cable TV at that time had Time Warner Cable. And everyone who had Time Warner Cable had the same gray Time Warner Cable box and the same gray Time Warner remote control. Not so interesting, except . . .

We figured out that if we aimed our own remote control through someone else's front window, we could change the station on them! Absolute TV power! And, yes, we *absolutely* used it. Again and again and again. We ran around the neighborhood, sneaking from one house to the next, changing people's stations or turning people's TVs on and off. They might be sitting on the couch, reading a book, and the TV would pop on, or they'd be eating dinner in front of the TV and it would click off. We thought we were hilarious.

We'd laugh as people tried to fix whatever problem they thought they might be having with their TV. They'd hit the remote, and we'd hit ours again. They'd hit their remote again, and we would hit ours again, and we'd go back and forth like this until the person gave up or we got bored and moved on to the next house. Like I said, we thought we were very funny. Actually, sometimes we thought we were *so* funny that we would laugh loud enough for someone to catch us, or not really catch us, but they'd come to the window and see four little clowns dressed in all black, laughing their heads off across their lawn.

They'd yell and they'd scream, maybe they'd come to the door. Sometimes they even called the police. And as police cars rolled into the neighborhood—one, maybe two—we'd dash off into the shadows. We'd hide under bushes for what felt like hours, though it was probably only ten minutes or so, as the cars slowly drove up and down the street.

Thing is, the cops never got out of the car. Nobody said anything through a megaphone. Nobody flashed any lights. Nobody was trying all that hard to find us. But still, we hid— because we imagined we were in the middle of some great adventure, pulling a fast one on the police and everybody else. *Whoa! Look what we did! We didn't even get caught. We even snuck past the cops!* This was our thirteen-year-old attitude. But one night the mission changed. Two of us got a little bolder.

Oh, wait. Hold up a second—I forgot to tell you something.

I actually didn't feel comfortable doing any of this. Every time we set out, I was nervous and definitely a little scared. Not only because I might get caught—I was also nervous and scared because what we were doing, we were doing to our *neighbors*. These were people I knew, people I delivered the newspaper to in the morning, people I raked leaves for in the fall or shoveled snow for in the winter, people I would see as I walked to and from school. Maybe they had an older kid or a younger kid I knew. These were people who, although we didn't have the word for it at the time, we were often terrorizing.

Imagine four people dressed in all black, just outside your

front window. No one knew who we were, no one knew how old we were, no one knew where we were coming from. We were scaring people in our costumes.

So—back to the story. Like I was saying, one night we went out again with a Time Warner Cable remote, and two of my friends went off to a neighbor's house farther up the hill, farther than we had gone before. They went to her back patio, and even though we usually only messed with the TV, this time they knocked on the window.

The older woman who lived alone was inside, near the window, and my friends scared the living @#&%? out of her! But what none of us knew at the time was that her son, or grandson—some man in his twenties—was also in the house.

And he came barreling out the front door.

Now, my friends who'd actually knocked on the window ran off behind the house. But the two of us who lagged behind, the two who had not scared the woman but were standing like two dumb cows chewing their cud in the middle of the street under a streetlight (under a STREETLIGHT!), had no idea what our friends had done. The guy who'd just burst through the front door saw us standing there like a pair of idiots. And he made a beeline for us. My buddy took off and got away. I did not.

The man grabbed me and swung me around. "What's your name?" he demanded. I didn't respond. He slammed me in the stomach, and I groaned. "What's your name?" he asked again.

"Brian Kelly," I said, trying to be clever, thinking that Brian Kelly and Brendan Kiely have nothing in common, right? He pulled the T-shirt (my "ninja mask") off my head, and as he did so, lights began flickering on over the front stoops and front doors of other houses along the street.

"Did you finally catch one of them?" someone yelled.

People I knew, people who knew my family, people who knew me, people who knew my younger brother, people who knew my parents—that's who lived in the neighborhood. The parents from one of the houses—where the family of one of my brother's friends lived, in fact—shouted, "Who is it?"

Now, earlier that summer I had gone to an overnight wilderness camp—one of those camps with a collection of cabins near the edge of a lake where kids like me learned to shoot an arrow from a bow and scramble across rope bridges in a canopy of trees. And because it was an overnight camp and my mother didn't want me to lose my clothes or have someone else take them, she'd ironed name tags onto the inside collar of everything . . . including my black "ninja mask."

So back on the street, after the guy had slammed me in the stomach a second time, he caught a glimpse of that name tag glowing like a firefly under the streetlamp. "Brian Kelly?" he grumbled. Then he turned to the parents of my brother's friend: "It's Brendan Kiely."

"We know him. Calling his father right now," the dad responded.

There was a lot more yelling and name-calling after that, but now that I'd been caught and my parents would find out, somehow that meant that everything was over for the night. The guy let me go.

Didn't matter, though. I knew I was doomed at home.

There was nothing worse in my mind than having my father find out what I'd done. That night, after he was done yelling at me, my father explained to me that we were going to go to that woman's house the next day and apologize.

"But, *Dad*," I protested. "Dad, I didn't do anything. I wasn't holding the remote, I was never the one who was changing stations on people. I didn't go up to that woman's window and knock on it. It wasn't me. I didn't do anything. I shouldn't be the one in trouble. It was Chris and Sean."

"Did you tell them that what they were going to do was a bad idea?"

"Um. No."

"Did you try to stop them, at all, any of those nights you were out there with them?"

"Um. No."

"Later, after one or two of those first nights out, did you say to them, 'Hey, guys, let's not do this anymore'?"

"Um. No."

"Then, Brendan, you're just as guilty as they are. You didn't try to stop them. It makes you an accomplice, in fact."

Wait, whaaat?

Yup.

My father explained that I didn't have to be the one holding the remote. I didn't have to be the one knocking on the window. I didn't have to be the one scaring someone in my neighborhood, making someone in my neighborhood feel unsafe, to still share some of the responsibility. Basically, I didn't have to be the one who had done *any* of the damage to still be part of the problem.

≈ ≈ ≈

And now you're probably wondering, *What the heck does any of this have to do with white privilege? Isn't that what we're supposed to be talking about here?*

Follow me a second.

All that "ninja" stuff? If I allow my friends to do the harming, then I'm just like them. I'm dressed in the same costume. I'm hiding in the same shadows. I'm doing the same thing.

But I didn't do it!

Hmmm.

But, because I didn't stop it . . .

I allowed it.

Which meant I went along with it.

And it'd be the exact same thing if a friend, say, told a racist joke or made a racist comment. Or if one of the adults in my life was doing something racist, like always picking on the Navajo kid in class or making fun of the way some of the Mexican kids' parents pronounced words in English.

If I don't say anything in situations like this, I might as well be doing what they're doing. Just like with the remote control, I don't have to have my finger on the button—I don't have to be the one saying or doing those things. But if I stand by and let it happen, let other people harm others, scare others, act in racist ways, or say racist things . . . then I'm going along with that racism.

I didn't do it!

But I went along with it.

Which means I enabled it.

Which also means I now need to take some responsibility for it.

Here's the thing about racism. For way too long, way too many white people—even if they weren't outright saying and doing racist things—were staying silent, were standing by and letting it happen. Were enabling it.

So now it is on us, people who are white like me, to not keep making that same mistake. To speak out about it. To try to stop it when we see it or hear it. By doing that, we can take some of the responsibility for it.

That's on us white people.

I think we *want* to do it . . .

But now we really *must* do it.

I'll start by speaking out about it myself—against myself. Because maybe you're thinking, *Hey, what about the four-white-kids-dressed-like-ninjas part of your story?* (At least I hope you were thinking that!) And see? I'm coming back to it, just like I promised.

So, maybe I'm pointing out the obvious, but four white boys pretending to be "ninjas"? This is what people are talking about when they're talking about cultural appropriation. We weren't ninjas; we were four white boys who dressed in all black and thought messing with our neighbors was funny. But cultural appropriation isn't funny. It's taking what is a piece of another person's culture and twisting it around into something shallow and one dimensional for your own amusement. Whether it's for Halloween, a theme party, or any other occasion (um, any of your favorite or local teams use names like Braves, or Indians, or—seriously—Chiefs? And what do the mascots look like?), reducing people from another culture, especially one that is marginalized in my community—what did we know about Japanese culture?—to a costume is just plain wrong. Because by reducing a culture down to a costume, and doing so repeatedly, there's a danger that I'll begin to think of people I meet from that culture as only what I associate with that costume.

For example, I've heard many people of East Asian descent explain—whether they're from Japan or Korea or China or elsewhere—that they often get teased by white people for *either* knowing *or* not knowing a martial art! And that "teasing" is often followed by further racist comments. Saying nasty, degrading stuff about foods and smells and accents, or about being dirty, or about carrying diseases. Or about "who is supposed to be in this country" and "who isn't." Or about who is "supposed" to be good at math or science. Or stuff that is just so mean and cruel about people's bodies.

All of it is racist.

All of it "begins as a joke" but slides so quickly into an overall attitude one person has toward another entire group of people (um, that's called "racism"). That's why just putting on a costume for an event can be the beginning of a very slippery slope to doing something much worse. Changing the pitch of our voice, making certain bodily gestures, slipping into "character" that's really just caricature—all of it is racist. Other people aren't just costumes and caricatures, and reducing someone to a caricature really hurts.

See what I'm saying? Why even begin going down this inevitable road to hurting someone else? Why take the time to double down on that hurt by defending your "right" to be able to do so?

Sure. We do have the right . . . to be a jerk! But, honest question: Why does anyone want to be a jerk so badly?

Here's another example of how jokes slide so easily into racism:

I was in a bar—hey, I'm an adult, what can I tell you? I was out with a few coworkers. There were four guys sitting around a table: three of us were white, and one was Black. Now, we're all sitting around telling stories and laughing and joking and having a fine time until one of the white guys starts telling a story about a neighbor who got mad at him. And once he got rolling with his story, he started acting out *how* his neighbor was telling him off. His neighbor was a Black woman, and this white man thought it would be funnier if he "slipped into character" as he told his story. He changed his voice. He over-emphasized his facial expressions. He exaggerated his head movements and hand gestures.

Oh, no, I thought. *This is terrible.* I just wanted him to stop. *Please stop. Please stop. Pleasestop-pleasestop-pleasestop.* And when I realized he wasn't going to, I started to muster up some courage. I tried to interrupt him, but he just talked over me. I tried again, but it was like a whisper in my throat, and he kept going. I was trying to interrupt, but I was also trying to be polite because I didn't want to make a scene or make the one Black person at the table have to explain to the man's face why he was being so racist. But I was just acting too slowly, too quietly, too . . . not enough-ly!

Then the Black man, who was sitting beside me, started whacking my leg with his, as if he were tapping out our own kind of secret Morse code, saying, *What the hell is wrong with you, Brendan? Shut this idiot up!*

And so I did. I shouted over him and told him to drop the acting.

I didn't have to tell him why. He looked at the Black man sitting across from him and realized instantly how much he'd hurt his colleague—by "just trying to be funny."

But dig a little deeper.

To where the harder question lies.

If this was how the white man saw his neighbor . . . how did he see his colleague across the table?

Just like my father had explained to me about those late-night "ninja missions" . . .

I wasn't the one putting on this racist one-man show in the bar. But if I let it keep going? If I didn't stop it from happening, I was enabling the racist story to keep on being racist— and therefore causing more and more and more harm to my friend at the table, not to mention anyone else in my life who would have been hurt by this.

And you know what else?

Although I definitely cannot claim to be hurt by that caricaturing in the same way that my Black colleague was, I *can* be offended by it. I *was* offended by it—because *it was* offensive!

It was offensive, and it flat-out hurt a person right there

at the table with me. And if I'd allowed it to keep happening, I'd be just another person in that group enabling harm to others.

To put it bluntly: I had to take some responsibility and shut that sh-t down, because if I *didn't* do precisely that, I'd be part of the group doing the harm.

And you know what *else* else?

What if it had been just the three of us white guys when my colleague told his story? Would I have stopped him? I hope so. I still should have. In fact, that's just as important: to point out the harm of racism, even if it is only other white people around the table.

Because that's the point here. One thing that is often hard for us white people to admit is that we are part of a group—a group that has done harm to other people.

Ever hear a white person say, "But I didn't create slavery. I didn't own any slaves"? Or, "I didn't push native people from their homes"? Probably far, far too many times. I know I have. Many white people—news anchors, TV personalities, blog authors—say those kinds of things, and you know what? Every time one of us says things like that, those lines land like slurs and insults on the people whose families have been deeply hurt by slavery and displacement.

Sometimes you hear things so many times, you find yourself saying something like it too. But here's the thing about the language that we use:

The language we use affects our attitudes.

Our attitudes affect our behavior.

Our behavior has an enormous impact on the lives of other people around us.

When my friends and I were setting out on our "ninja runs"—okay, enough, let's just call them what they were, because we certainly were *not* ninjas—when my friends and I were setting out on our white-boy runs (white-boy antics, really), we said to one another, "It's no big deal. We're not doing anything wrong. We're not hurting anyone." That was our language.

When we were moving lawn furniture and switching people's TV stations, we weren't saying it out loud, but we were thinking, *No big deal, not doing anything wrong, not hurting anyone.* That was our attitude.

But what was our behavior? We did all those things in our neighborhood on our white-boy runs, and the people we did them to had to scramble to the door in confusion or climb to the top of their garage and collect their patio furniture—they could have fallen, broken a bone, or worse. People had to move their potted flowers back to the right location and feel uneasy that someone had been on their property in the middle of the night . . . they had to wonder, *What might that someone do next?* People got scared out of their minds when they saw guys dressed all in black knocking on their window.

Our white-boy runs behavior affected people's lives. And *not* in a good way.

Our language. Our attitudes. Our actions. We were responsible for all of it. What if one or two of us had stood up and said, before it all got started, *No. This IS a big deal. This is wrong. We are hurting people if we do this?* Far fewer people would have been scared, annoyed, and potentially put in dangerous situations.

The same holds true with race, with racism, and with white privilege, too.

Here's how:

What if a group of white people in your city or town said, "We don't want any Black people moving here," and they worked really hard to make that happen? Now, you might not have been part of the group that *actively* tried to stop Black people from moving in—but if you knew about it, did you try to stop them? If you knew and didn't try, then you have to own it. You are just as responsible.

Or what if a group of white politicians went so far as to say they didn't want any people coming into the United States from a list of seven countries where the majority population is Muslim? Did *you* actually sit down and try to get that bill passed through Congress? Probably not. But if you knew the politicians were talking about doing it, did you write letters to Congress to tell them how hurtful this would be to our Muslim neighbors living beside us? Did you stand in the street with a sign saying that the proposed Muslim ban was racist?

Those, by the way, are two real-life examples.

All across America white real estate agents have been blatantly discriminating against Black people for decades. So have the people who've supported their discrimination by not objecting to it. And that's not just "something that happened in the past"—it's still going on. Real estate agents in Long Island, New York, got caught discriminating in 2019. And in 2017, President Donald Trump signed an executive order that effectively banned all people from seven majority Muslim countries from coming into our country—including refugees who were fleeing war.

All of this is real.

Who *did* get to move into the homes in those towns on Long Island? Who *did* get let into the country? You guessed it—white people. Remember when we were talking about how racism isn't only about denial and disadvantage, but also about who is *given* the advantage?

When I got caught on the white-boy run, I sure as heck did not want to be held accountable. I wanted someone to absolve me of any guilt, without even having to admit that I'd done anything wrong. *I didn't do anything!* And when I put it like that, it becomes clear to me that that is exactly what many of us white people do when it comes to conversations about racism in America. We want to be told, *But not you!* We want to be let off the hook without ever having to admit that we've done anything wrong in the first place.

It's the admitting that we are part of something wrong that we stumble over. And then we feel funny when someone tells us that we, too (even though we didn't think so), are part of that group doing something wrong.

Bizarrely, it was a white supremacist I met in Madison, Wisconsin, who taught me the uncomfortable truth about what group I really belong to in this country.

And that's a story I really need to tell you about.

(PS: And like an electric shock biting my fingers and zipping through me to the ends of my hairs, it was a reminder of just how much my own white privilege can look a lot like white supremacy itself.)

(PPS: *And* all the more reason why I can—and must!—speak up and act out against it.)

Hard Look in the Mirror

Wait a second.

Before I get into it, I should tell you that after Jason Reynolds and I met and became friends, and we talked about racism and white privilege and The Talk some kids have to get—the "never got a talk" stuff that applied to me—he and I cowrote a novel called *All American Boys*. In it, a young Black man experiences police brutality and a young white man witnesses it. The story is about each of them figuring out who they are after it. After our book came out, we spent a lot of time traveling the country together talking about the book.

And I gotta tell you: One of my absolute favorite parts of my life as an author is visiting schools. I love it. I love chopping it up with you all after my presentation. I love hearing your reactions to what I had to say. I love the way you all so often challenge me—make me think harder. I love laughing and joking with you, and I love listening to you tell me what you care about and why it's so important.

So after any presentation I give at a school, I hang around so that students can come talk to me one-on-one. It was the same deal in Madison, Wisconsin.

In fact, Jason and I were there together, and after the presentation we hung around the gym, each talking to a different small group of students. Jason and his group slowly made their way to the exit, but I remained behind because as my group got smaller and smaller, I could see one kid hanging off to the side, waiting so she could be the last one to talk to me—I assumed it had to be important. Sure enough, my group steadily dwindled away until it was only her still there, a high school senior, a young white woman.

We were the only two people left in the entire gym.

Her hand shook as she lifted her finger and pointed it at my face. "You're not white," she said. "You're not white on the inside."

For a second I thought I'd misheard her. What the heck was she talking about? On the *inside*?

Then I felt my nerves spark. *Oh nooooo. This is going to be bad.*

She then just started dropping one wild statement after another about the "greatness" of white people. About how white people had discovered everything in the field of science (which is wrong). About how all inventions were pioneered by white people (wrong again). About the *superiority* of white people (SO wrong!)—and when I heard *that*, I figured I'd been respectful long enough. I interrupted her. Not only because everything she was saying was BS—and it was *all* BS; none of it was true—but also because my uneasiness had boiled over into deep anger.

I didn't know what to say. It's like talking to a person who is pointing up to the sky on a bright summer day and shouting about how great the snowflakes are. Hello! There are no snowflakes! It's ninety degrees out here. What the @#&%? are you talking about?

But I kept my anger to myself, and I told her that I felt bad for her that someone had fed her so much wildly deluded information and made her believe it. And that really *was* who I was most mad at, not at her, but at the adults who'd messed her up in this way.

And *then* I got to wondering: How did she act in school? Here she was *saying* awful things about Black people and additional people of the Global Majority to me, so what did she actually *do* in school every day around the very people she was clearly so prejudiced against?

And now I was worrying for the safety of the students in the school who were not white.

And THEN my fears and insecurities took a whole different turn. I started to worry about me. I started to think, *Man, I hope no one looks at me and thinks I'm anything like her. I hope EVERYone knows I'm nothing like her. Because I'm nothing like her, right? I mean, right? Please tell me I'm right! PLEASEpleaseplease!!!*

So, okay, freeze the frame midscene here.

Now, yes, of course, this white supremacist and I don't have a lot in common. We have completely different worldviews. Mine is based in reality, and hers? I don't know, it's like it's from another—

But wait! Wait! See what I did just there? The way I tried to create this massive difference and distance between her and me? Like I'm one of "these" kinds of white people and she's one of "those" kinds of white people?

That was exactly what she'd been saying to me when she first started speaking. She'd tried to "disown" me as a white person. *You're not white. You're not white on the inside.* And then here I was trying to "disown" her. *You're just one of the fringe white people. You're just one of those "bad apples." You're not like the rest of us.*

Ugh. That white supremacist and I were actually doing the same thing. We were both looking at the other person and thinking about how different we were from each other.

And that's when it hit me.

Now unfreeze the frame.

And the scene unfolds, because I glanced across the empty gym and saw a couple of teachers who'd poked their heads back through the doorway, looking over at us. What did they see? They saw two white people having a conversation.

Two white people who, no matter how much we disagreed with each other, no matter how different we felt from each other, still experienced life similarly in all too many ways. For example:

- No matter what kind of car she or I drove, nobody made any assumptions about

whether or not the car might be stolen
simply by looking at us.
• No matter who we pass on the sidewalk,
they rarely clutch their purse or wallet out
of instant fear at our approach.
• No matter where we bought Band-Aids,
we could always find some that matched
our skin tone.
• No matter what our behavior was in
school, we were four times less likely
to get suspended than Black and Latinx
students.
• No matter what toy store we walked into,
we could be sure to find a doll in our
likeness.
• No matter how many TV shows we've
watched or streamed or binged, we can
always find yet another with only or
mostly characters who look like us.
• No matter what store we walked into
at the mall, we could be fairly confident
we would not be watched or followed or
harassed.

This list of common experiences, or privileges, the white
supremacist and I share? It just keeps growing and growing
and growing.

Because we 100 percent share white privilege.

There really isn't a "those" white people and a "these" white people—not in terms of white privilege. All white people share the same privileges, the same advantages, of white living.

The girl from Madison (and she could have been from any-where—Tulsa, Cheyenne, Tampa, Pittsburgh, Everytown, USA) might have agreed with the white Uber driver whose gun I sat on in Baton Rouge.

She might have agreed with the white men who walked onto an elevator with me and Jason one time in South Carolina and started dropping the N-word in front of him and the Black woman in the elevator with us.

She might have agreed with the white boy who started chanting "Blue Lives Matter" in an auditorium in Philadelphia crowded mostly with Black and additional people of the Global Majority.

No matter how much she might have agreed with "those" white people I've met among my travels in America, and no matter how much I might disagree with "those" white people, she and I both walk around the world living white.

Whether I like it or not, I'm privileged in all the same ways as a white supremacist—at least at first glance.

It is all too seductive for white people who aren't white supremacists to want to distance themselves from white supremacists. We think (wildly!): *That's not me! That's not me! I hope no one from the Global Majority looks at me and thinks I'm anything like her. I'm not!* But there's something not quite right about this. By saying that, it makes it easier for me to weasel out of taking any responsibility. I'm basi-cally saying that racism is the white supremacist's fault, not mine—*and so I don't have to take any responsibility for it.*

And, yup, when that's my attitude, I'm actually part of the problem.

Which makes me a lot more like that white supremacist in Madison than I ever would have thought.

In fact, more like her than I'm really comfortable with.

So who needs to take responsibility for that white supremacist?

I take a hard look in the mirror and say, *Brendan, you need to be responsible for her.*

All of us white people need to be responsible for that white supremacist. We need to take some responsibility for the violent language in the elevator in South Carolina. We need to take some responsibility for the profound misunderstanding about the dignity and sacredness of human life when people are shouting "Blue Lives Matter."

"Responsibility," Brendan? Isn't that a bit much?

No. It's what my father was trying to get me to understand after he found out about the white-boy runs.

Too many of us white people let all the racism around us just slide. We give it a pass. We don't confront it . . .

And therefore it continues. When we let it slide, it gives permission for others to let it slide too, and then others to mimic that behavior, and still others to even escalate it.

But it doesn't *have* to be that way. We can take some of the responsibility so that we can help change some of the damage and injustice done by racism.

What if we made that a priority in our lives, like our nightly prayers maybe, or thought about it as often as we checked Instagram or TikTok, so it burned like a candle in the window of our hearts all the time? Like, 24/7. Not just for an hour. Not just after some public incident that's all over everyone's news feeds. Not just for a week, as though we were "responsibility tourists." Like we take a quick trip to the land of responsibility, snap a few photos, post a few rants on social media, but then check back out for the rest of our lives—or at least until we decide to mosey on back to the land of responsibility, when we're in the mood (or feeling a little extra guilty).

What does that mean?

For too many of us, that Uber driver is someone we work with. For too many of us, the guys dropping the N-word in the elevator are kids we go to school with. For too many of us, the people talking about how blue lives matter are sitting around our kitchen table having dinner with us.

Those kinds of comments are flying around *everywhere*. Just ask any person of the Global Majority in the United States if they've ever heard racist comments made about them to their face or in their presence. Those. Comments. Are. Everywhere. And they aren't just floating in the air like smoke drifting from some distant fire.

Someone lit the spark. Someone stoked the flame.

White people, we've done that.

Whether it is a comment in the lunchroom cafeteria or it is the rigged system denying textbooks . . .

. . . or starving some school systems of the money needed for proper supplies . . .

. . . or the history of segregation . . .

. . . or the practices of real estate brokers that have caused differences in property values that are the reason for unequal funds for school districts . . .

. . . or the way government officials have worked to deny people of the Global Majority their voting rights, so that they can't vote into power the people who want to make all the systemic changes to correct some of these injustices.

All of that is racism. Therefore, all of it results in white privilege.

And it's time to fight back against all that racism.

It's time to fight back against all that white privilege.

We can start now. Today. In that cafeteria, in that elevator, at the kitchen table—shutting down the jokes and the smarmy comments. Shutting down the language before the attitude grows and grows and becomes the behavior that is so dangerous. We can work against our own white privilege, because if we don't fight against it, we're supporting it.

It's like with a bully, right? No, I might not be the bully, but if I don't step in and try to stop the bully, if I don't make a loud and public stink about the bully's unacceptable behavior, if I just let him keep coming after someone again and again and again, then I gotta wonder: *Why am I giving the bully a pass instead of helping the person he's going after?*

And from the perspective of the person he's picking on, if I just stand there silently, it's damn clear I'm on the bully's team, not theirs.

That's the deal with racism and white privilege. Way, way too many white people look too much like we're on the racists' team, because not nearly enough of us are stepping up and speaking out about them.

So what, exactly, are the rest of us white people (those of us who aren't stepping up and speaking out) *doing* as we witness this bullying again and again and don't do anything to stop it?

Actually? This is a question I think a brilliant and courageous thirteen-year-old in Wellesley, Massachusetts, named Yusuf was trying to get us to think about.

But first . . .

Interruption

Now, what that girl in Wisconsin said to me is so bonkers and batsh-t wrong, I think it's absolutely necessary to interrupt myself here to say a couple of things.

Because some other things need to be said.

Remember how I said that The Talk about survival in the face of racism is also about pride? Well, here are some things that the girl from Wisconsin *didn't* know, but if she did, maybe they'd expand her understanding of who can and needs to be better celebrated in our country's past *and* our present . . . stories and biographies that so many of us white people ought to know about (and celebrate!) but don't.

Ever heard of Robert Smalls? I sure hadn't until only a couple years ago. Well, he was a Black man who, in a daring mission, snuck himself and seventeen other enslaved people past Confederate naval ships at the height of the Civil War, delivered them all to freedom, and later, after the war, served in the US House of Representatives. He founded the Republican Party of South Carolina. In South Carolina today there are over one hundred public spaces adorned with monuments honoring well-known white Confederates. (In fact, there are more than fifteen hundred public monuments and memorials to prominent Confederates and the Confederacy across the entire United States.)

Robert Smalls didn't get his own until 2013.

That is the point here.

How many more stories like Robert Smalls's would Americans know if there were more monuments like his in every state? In other words, whose history have we chosen to keep alive and why? And who makes these decisions?

I bet you can guess.

What would it mean to *all of us* in our country if we took the time to honor some of the people whose stories seem to have been nearly forgotten?

People like:

- **Richard Allen**, a Black man who, born into slavery, bought his own freedom in the 1780s, then started the first Black church in America in 1787 in an old blacksmith's shop, because the church he previously joined in Philadelphia, St. George's Church, imposed segregated seating.

- **Mary Ellen Pleasant**, a Black woman who eventually became known as the "Mother of Civil Rights in California." Though her origins in the 1810s are disputed—she may have been born free in Philadelphia or as a slave in Georgia—she was later indentured to a shopkeeper in Nantucket, then married a wealthy landowner and, once widowed, made her way to San Francisco. With tenacity and a sharp business mind, she amassed an estimated fortune of $30 million (an astonishing amount of money in our time, let alone hers), then used her wealth and power for abolitionist causes and civil rights legal cases. (What a life! How do we all not know about her? Where's her biopic? This woman is truly amazing!!)

- **Mary Fields**, also born into slavery, who, once free, at the age of sixty-three, became the first Black person to work for the US Postal Service because she was the fastest applicant for the job to hitch a team of six horses.

- **Lewis Latimer**, the son of slaves, who would go on to draft the patent drawings for Alexander

Graham Bell's telephone and who later improved Thomas Edison's invention of the light bulb. Until Latimer's contribution, the bulb stayed lit for only a couple days, but by extending its life much longer, Latimer paved the way for Edison's Electric Light Company. He also cowrote the very first book on electric lighting, titled *Incandescent Electric Lighting* (1890).

Or fast-forward to more modern times:

- **Macario Garcia**, who was the first Mexican immigrant to be awarded the Medal of Honor, the highest military decoration in the United States, in 1943.

- **Dr. Kazue Togasaki**, who was one of the first Japanese American women to become a medical doctor in the United States but who had to travel a long way to get there. After witnessing the devastation of the 1906 earthquake in San Francisco, Togasaki worked to become a nurse, and although she graduated first in her class, she couldn't find employment because, in her own words, "they didn't use Japanese nurses." Later, during World War II, she was forcibly interned at an American-run Japanese incarceration center, where she safely delivered fifty babies. After the war she went on to start her own medical practice and delivered ten thousand more babies before she retired at the age of seventy-five.

- **Kiyoshi Kuromiya**, a Japanese American author and activist who was actually born in one of those Japanese incarceration centers and who dedicated his life to fighting for civil rights. He befriended Dr. Martin Luther King Jr. and, after King's assassination, helped look after his children. Kuromiya later went on to become a prominent figure of the LGTBQ+ movement.

- **Sylvia Mendez**, a woman of Mexican and Puerto Rican descent who, at only eight years old, played a pivotal role in desegregating the "whites-only" and "Mexican" schools of California in the 1940s. She then set the precedent for further desegregation legislation during the civil rights movement of the 1950s and '60s, when her family sued and won their case that school segregation was unconstitutional because it violated the Fourteenth Amendment, which guarantees all US citizens "equal protection of the laws."

- **Albert Baez**, a Mexican American (and father of Joan Baez) who, as a physicist and inventor, developed the first X-ray microscopes.

- **Bayard Rustin**, a Black man who organized and strategized the 1963 March on Washington, but remained in the shadows because he was gay and had ties to communism.

- **Dolores Huerta**, a Mexican American who cofounded the Agricultural Workers Association in 1960 and the National Farm Workers Association in 1962 and was awarded the first-ever Eleanor Roosevelt Award for Human Rights in 1998 from President Bill Clinton. She also received the Presidential Medal of Freedom from President Barack Obama in 2012.

- **Larry Itliong**, who emigrated from the Philippines in 1929, when he was only sixteen years old—and after working as a migrant farmer for years—became a heavily influential labor organizer. And though Cesar Chavez often gets the most notice for it, Itliong was the original coordinator of the initial actions that became the famous Delano Grape Strike of the 1960s.

- **Marsha P. Johnson**, a Black trans woman and activist at the leading edge of the LGTBQ+ movement.

- **Wilma Mankiller**, who was the first woman to serve as Principal Chief of the Cherokee Nation and who received the Presidential Medal of Freedom from President Bill Clinton in 1998.

- **Mohammad S. Hamdani**, a Pakistani American man who was killed while rescuing victims of the September 11, 2001, attacks at the World Trade Center.

And there are so many others still shaping our culture today, among them:

- **Mae Jemison**, who's not only the first Black woman astronaut to go into outer space, but who continues to work to inspire and facilitate career paths for young women of the Global Majority by promoting opportunities to get more involved in technology, math, and engineering careers.

- **LaDonna Harris**, a member of the Comanche Nation, who is the founder and president of Americans for Indian Opportunity and who cochaired the Women's March on Washington.

- **Fazlur Rahman Khan**, a Bangladeshi American known as the "Einstein of structural engineering," who designed the Willis Tower (well, I still call it the Sears Tower) in Chicago, the tallest building in America at the time it was built.

- **Faisal Alam**, a Pakistani American man who founded the Al-Fatiha Foundation, dedicated to advocating for the rights and lives of gay, lesbian, and transgender Muslims.

- **Dr. David Ho**, a Taiwanese American who was one of the very first doctors to study and understand AIDS and has continued to lead groundbreaking research, including work on COVID-19.

Just like all the other lists in this book, these could go on and on too. But be honest. How many of these people have you heard of? And yet, shouldn't we know them? Shouldn't they receive monuments? Plaques? Be highlighted in our history books?

We *know* who's made the decision to keep them out. But we can also decide to more publicly and prominently honor them. Robert Smalls finally got his monument in 2013. Who else should we be celebrating?

What Bullying
Looks Like . . . to a
Whole Community

Speaking of cheering people on, I want to tell you about a kid named Yusuf in Massachusetts.

Remember how I said Jason and I often traveled together and spoke at schools after we cowrote *All American Boys* together? Well, one of those stops was in Wellesley, Massachusetts.

We gave our presentation to the school and did our best to be as honest as we could about how and why we wrote it. As usual, after the presentation we took questions from the crowd. And, as usual, the students, in this case eighth graders, had a whole host of fascinating questions for us, from how our own personal lives influenced the book to why we ended it the way we did (have to read it to find out—ha!). Also as usual, the young people were inspiring, and they offered powerful challenges.

But something different happened at this visit.

Yusuf, who, like most of his classmates, had been slumped down in his chair as if he were melting into it, suddenly stood and began to ask a question about the parallels between racism and religious discrimination. His voice shook, he was nervous (also like most of his classmates when they asked questions), but his eyes widened as he found energy and enthusiasm and continued speaking. He wanted Jason and me, and everyone in the room, to know what it was like for him—someone who was not white, who was not Black, who was not the target of police brutality—to be threatened, terrorized really, by his own neighbors and peers because of his Muslim faith. He was a young Muslim whose family and community had been threatened in spring 2017. He asked us if we thought religion, and his in particular, gets all tangled up with racism.

He told us about the white kids who rode by his house on bicycles and threw cans of pork and beans at it. Tears began to roll down his cheeks, but with steadfast courage, he went on. He told us about the note nailed to the front door of his mosque that read: *There is a new sheriff in town, and his name is Donald Trump.* It also said that the new sheriff would clear Muslims out of the country. Later he even showed us a photograph of the note.

Yusuf, his family, and his cultural community were being terrorized by white people. Targeted specifically because of the cultural group they belonged to—because they were Muslim.

Yusuf shared his story with us because he saw a connection between the harassment of Black people by police and the violent threats his family was facing. Cultural bullying wasn't new for Yusuf—he'd moved to Massachusetts from South Africa when he was ten years old, and he'd known what it was like to be teased and harassed for who he was since he'd arrived. But the sheer *publicness* of this new threat had taken things to a whole other level, and the note about the new sheriff in town was a direct assault on his community.

This anti-Muslim sentiment isn't racist, *exactly* (there are white people who are Muslim, for example), but it functions the same way racism does. And anti-Muslim violence in the United States, in particular, is so often directed at people whose families hail from Africa, the Middle East, and Asia and who, in the United States, often do not identify as, nor are "seen" or "perceived" as, white. In other words, this anti-Muslim violence and hate is predominantly directed at people of the Global Majority who are Muslim. And the anti-Muslim hate spills over into racism directed toward people of all faiths and backgrounds from those same parts of the world. So it's anti-Muslim and racist intertwined together.

This anti-Muslim, anti–Middle Eastern, anti–Central

Asian, and anti–South Asian attitude and behavior is very much like the anti–East Asian attitude and behavior that has been around for a long time and exploded recently during the COVID-19 pandemic.

As I mentioned before, although Irish immigrants faced their own kind of opposition in America for some time, that opposition melted away as soon as Irish people, and Americans of Irish descent, were seen as (perceived to be) "white." Like the Germans and the Swedes and the Poles and many other immigrants from Europe and the Mediterranean, Irish immigrants who made a new life in America over time "became white." Remember, immigrant groups like the Irish and Germans and many other non-Anglo-Saxon ethnicities were not "seen as" or included within "white." But in a relatively short period of time people of all those European ethnic origins "became white" (were "seen as" or "included within" the racial group "white") in America.

See again how "race"—in this context, "white"—is totally made up?!

And by "becoming white," these groups could begin to take advantage of white privilege. One of the ways they did so was to claim that they "belonged here" whereas immigrants from Asia did not.

And the American legal system (ah, see again why it's called "systemic racism"?) was on their side—encouraging immigration from Europe and discouraging it from Asia. How? Well, again, one really impactful way was the Chinese Exclusion Act (mentioned earlier) that President Chester A. Arthur signed into law in 1882.

It *denied* immigration rights to people from China (and all over Asia). And it *advantaged* immigration rights to people from European countries. One place in particular was Norway.

Get this:

Between 1870 and 1910 (same time as the Chinese Exclusion Act) an entire quarter—yes, a whole 25 percent!—of the working-age population of Norway emigrated to find better work. And, yessiree, most of them came to the good old US of A, where work—work legally denied to people from Asia or taken away from deported people of Mexican and Latin American descent—was more plentiful and better paying than in Norway.

So whenever there is a conversation about all immigration to the United States being a "level playing field," *remember the Norwegians!* (*That* is a sentence I never thought I'd write.) Remember that they were given access to opportunity in America, *welcomed* into America. They were *not* rounded up and deported, they were *not* blocked from entering the country like so many other people were—namely, people from parts of the world west and south of the USA. The Norwegians were given an advantage. And the Norwegians weren't alone.

But history lives in the present.

Because in 2018, President Donald Trump stated that he wished more immigrants in the United States were from countries like Norway, not from, as he described them, "sh-thole countries." His disparaging comments about these countries came only one year after he signed the executive order known as the "Muslim Ban," which froze or severely limited immigration from Syria, Iran, Iraq, Sudan, Yemen, Libya, and Somalia.

So the question of who "belongs" in the United States has always been a racist question, a question that reinforces white privilege and targets people who are not *perceived* to be white.

I mean, never once did people make assumptions about who I was or whether I "belonged" here in the United States. And the twisted irony of "white living" is that when families like mine started to be seen mostly as "white" and less and less as Irish or Polish or Italian or *Norwegian*, our whiteness did in fact lump all of us, from all our different cultural backgrounds, into one *perceived* racial group. White.

But the effect of that erasing of cultural distinctions didn't harm white people, as it did Vincent Chin, who we talked about earlier, and as it has for so many people of East Asian, South Asian, Arab, and Middle Eastern cultural backgrounds in the United States. Instead, that erasure into "white" granted advantages . . . the advantages of white living.

However, lumping people with cultural backgrounds from places as diverse and different as Pakistan, India, Bangladesh, Sri Lanka, Syria, and Egypt, perceiving them to be, profiling them all as "Muslim"—and then being prejudiced (another good word here would be "bigoted") by thinking that being Muslim somehow makes you *dangerous*—that *does* affect people's lives. It's called "racial profiling," and it damages psyches and endangers lives.

Racial profiling assumes a person from a racial or ethnic group is already guilty of something, or about to do something wrong, or be untrustworthy in some way. And if you have a job in which you have to interact with a person you've racially profiled—say you're a cop or an airport official or a store clerk—and you act on what are only your *assumptions* about that person (not anything that person has actually done!), then your racial profiling (um, your RACISM) can deeply affect that person's life.

With my whiteness, in contrast, it doesn't matter if I'm mistaken for British, French, Danish, or Hungarian. It has no impact on my life whatsoever. My whiteness has to some degree wiped out whatever meaning any of those ethnicities might have had; in America I'm white, at least as seen by others.

But for people in America of African, Middle Eastern, South Asian, and Middle Asian descent, being labeled as "potential terrorists" out of irrational fear and racist projections has a profound impact on the lives of thousands and thousands.

Language, as I mentioned, affects attitude, and attitude affects behavior—it's a chain reaction that, once in motion, is really hard to stop. So even if some comment begins as only a "joke" or general demeaning talk toward a group of people, that language can give rise to inaccurate or inappropriate assumptions and can inspire negatively charged attitudes toward those people that can in turn lead to violence against them.

Like this domino effect:

- In the 2016 presidential campaign and just after he was elected, Donald Trump made repeated inflammatory remarks about Muslims. (That's the language part.)

- Though his remarks were criticized by some people, members of his party and supporters of his presidential campaign did nothing to combat or denounce those remarks and, instead, encouraged them. (That's the attitude part.)

- From November 2016 to November 2017 hate crimes against South Asian, Muslim, Sikh, Hindu, Middle Eastern, and Arab communities increased by *46 percent*. (That's the behavior part.)

Or, as one community leader explained, "Deadly shootings, torched mosques, vandalized homes and businesses, and young people harassed at school have animated an acutely violent post-election year."

Similar to what Yusuf told all of us in the auditorium that day.

He wasn't only telling a truth about his family being bullied. He was telling a truth about his community in Massachusetts being bullied, and even a truth about a much broader, larger web of communities being bullied across the entire country.

And for people who are Muslim or are "perceived to be" Muslim, this is just as common today as it was after September 11, 2001.

As a New Yorker, I have heard dozens of stories from people who were lumped together into one single, deeply hurtful stereotype of a "terrorist" in the aftermath of the tragedy of

9/11. One that never stops gnawing at me is from a colleague at a media company I worked for at the time.

My colleague's family had emigrated from Sri Lanka when he was young, so he had grown up mostly in the United States. Although he'd experienced racism and bigotry because of his skin color and background throughout those years, as an adult he enjoyed his job in Manhattan, his married life, friends, and neighborhood in Brooklyn very much. But after 9/11 all that began to change. The FBI knocked on his door late one night. One of his neighbors had called them to say she believed there was a terrorist living in her building, and my colleague was interrogated by two agents in his very own hallway.

He was humiliated and angry. There was—of course!—no evidence of terrorism. He hadn't done anything to invite suspicion. There was no reason for the call to the FBI other than the deeply ignorant fear motivating his neighbor—she knew what he looked like, and that was enough for her to fearfully imagine that he might be a "Muslim terrorist."

In fact, he wasn't even Muslim! Not that that mattered, because no one who is Muslim should have to face that harassment and profiling in the first place.

Even though the agents were kind and apologetic, even though they knew there was nothing to the "tip" from the neighbor, it was explained to my colleague that they were obligated to follow through and investigate. They were embarrassed that they had to come knock on his door, that they had to embarrass *him*. Furthermore, they explained, they were following up on bogus leads—racial profiling—

all over the city. White people like his neighbor, and some people who were not white, were calling in similarly useless, racist "tips." They weren't tips—they were a huge waste of time and energy, and they were grossly unfair to people who'd been racially profiled.

The agents left that night, and my colleague thought that was the end of it. But they were called back again. And then again. And. Then. Yet. Again.

They were called if my colleague played his music too loud, if his neighbor spotted him walking down the hall—it didn't matter the circumstance. She called, the law followed up, and time and again my colleague was harassed.

The pain mounted. The harassment mounted. Until, like anyone trying to protect his sanity and personal safety, he decided he had to move. He left a job he loved, a home he loved, a neighborhood he loved, and a city he loved—all because of a neighbor's prejudice and ignorance.

As far as I know, no one dropped "tips" on the white neighbor. No one embarrassed her. She didn't have to leave her job. She didn't have to leave her neighborhood. She didn't have to leave her city.

She was in the wrong, and my colleague had to pay for it.

Which, if you remember, was exactly what my friend was warning his eight-year-old son about when he gave him The Talk. (See how this is all connected?)

As you might imagine, my colleague's story wasn't unique. Hate crimes against American Muslims and people of Arab, Middle Eastern, and South Asian descent increased from 354 (a number that's already awful) in the year 2000 to 1,501 in the year 2001, with most happening from September to December—in other words, right after September 11. And too many white US representatives, church leaders, and other community leaders encouraged this kind of Islamophobia by making racist statements and inflammatory anti-Muslim remarks in TV appearances, at town meetings, and during other community events.

Islamophobia was again on the rise in the year or so leading up to Yusuf's story about the "new sheriff in town." In 2016 there were a ton of personal stories being shared about "flying while Muslim" because Muslim passengers on flights all across the country were being escorted off airplanes at alarming rates:

> In fact, public acts of discrimination,
> especially against Muslims, have spiked
> along with Donald Trump's venomous
> campaign rhetoric in this election season.
> That, coupled with travelers' anxiety about
> the threat of terrorist attacks, has yielded
> repeated episodes of baseless suspicion on
> airplanes—in other words, profiling.

There was this whole campaign across the country back then that went like this, "If you see something, say something," but people too often ran with that idea in the wrong direction. Hence:

> Prodded to say something, passengers and
> airline personnel are quick to see something,

but too often what they've really seen is a
person whose skin color or attire or language
is a trigger for unfounded accusation.

In other words: racial profiling.

In only one word: racism.

Never once has anyone looked at me suspiciously when boarding a plane. Never once, even when I switched seats without asking on a half-empty flight, did anyone think it was suspicious that I wanted to sit next to the emergency exit. Airline staff and fellow passengers have, for the most part, always been courteous and tried to accommodate any needs I might have.

In other words: white privilege.

In only one word: whiteness.

Because I, as a white person, have never experienced racial profiling—that type of cultural bullying that all too many people in America who are not white know too well.

And this is what Yusuf knew in his heart the day he told his story to the whole auditorium. He knew the cultural bullying was wrong. After speaking up during our presentation he wanted to say more about it. With far more bravery than I could have mustered, he submitted a speech to his teachers and asked to read it at his eighth-grade graduation. In it he shared some of the same details he'd told us in the auditorium that day, but the speech went further as he reflected on how his experience affected his school and his peers:

This school has its ups and downs, it has its good sides, its bad sides, its racism, its discrimination, but at the same time it also has open arms, willing to help you with anything. It's a place where any kid can go to a teacher and get help and advice on anything they need. I'm grateful for this school; I'm grateful for my life. This world isn't always great, especially with everything that's been going on recently: racism, terrorism, hatred, and shootings. But we need to be there for each other, to support each other. We don't know how people will react to certain things, how the small jokes we say can make someone go home and sob. We need to take care of our community. For every kid who gets bullied, it's not okay. For every kid who bullies, it's not okay. And for every kid who watches and doesn't do anything, it's not okay. I was that kid. I know what it's like to hear those small jokes made about you; they add up, they affect you, and they push you down. Don't think that the words you speak don't impact other people. Don't say, "It was just a joke" or "I didn't mean it." You did mean it; you said it. I hope all of us soon realize this. Like I said earlier, we need to be there for each other. For some people, we're all

they have, and if that's the case we need
to treat them like gems and support them.

I'm with you, Yusuf. Thank you for all that truth and courage.

13

So Step Up!

Yes! What Yusuf said! We need to be there for one another and stop all this bullying BS! Cut the racist crap!

Because now we know we have to learn the racist truth of our past to better see the racist truth of our present, and though we can't change the past, our history (*aaarrrrggghhh!*), we *can* change our present . . . our now.

So what do we do?

Because we have to do something!

Because unless I stand up and *do* something, I'm helping the people I claim to disagree with. The people I claim not to be. The people I don't *want* to be. It has nothing to do with what I *say* I believe or what I *say* is right or wrong. It has everything to do with what I'm actually *doing*.

So let's talk about what we can do to step up, white people. Let's *DO* it.

Time to step ^up!

14

Well, Actually, Hang on a Second . . . Step Back

Hold up, hold up. Forgot to tell you something. Before we do that—before white people step up—there's some other stuff we need to do first.

Cue the groaning. I know. I know.

But here's the deal: Have you ever wanted to do something really good, like help someone in some way or another, but then, when you did, it didn't work out the way you imagined it would? Like maybe the person you thought you were going to "help" just ended up mad at you instead?

That has absolutely happened to me.

When I was in middle school, I had a hard time falling asleep sometimes—often, actually. And that was a problem because I had a job. Yup. A real job. I had to get up at five in the morning, every day, to deliver the *Boston Globe* to a whole bunch of people around my neighborhood (other end of the neighborhood from the white-boy runs), then shower and eat breakfast before I'd finally walk to school with a bunch of other guys from my neighborhood.

So I had to get some sleep—because five a.m. is *early*! And to help fall asleep, I told myself stories. Mostly hero stories. And, uh . . . oh, man, this is terribly embarrassing. I invented little stories in which I, of course, was the hero. Some of them were as dopey as me hitting the buzzer beater three-pointer to win the game for my basketball team, again and again and again. In my story we just happened to *always* be down by two points with only a few seconds left to play. Always! And somehow I'd have to shoot from the corner while falling out-of-bounds or make some other nearly impossible shot. Quite the hero, wasn't I? But some of the stories were bizarrely complicated. Like the school was taken over by people who wanted to kidnap some of the students, and I had to figure out a way to sneak us out of the school, or get the kidnappers locked up in the music room by themselves, or—remember, this was that time in my life when I was obsessed with ninjas—I'd somehow disarm one of the kidnappers with a reverse roundhouse or some other acrobatic kick and pin him against the wall and say something totally over-the-top and cliché like, *Nice try, a--hole.*

Completely ridiculous.

But the stories of me saving the day did help me fall asleep.

Why exactly am I telling you this embarrassing stuff?

Well, on p. 146, I just finished saying that we white people have to do something about all the racism in our country. And we do. . . . But what I also need to let you know is that I'm not saying that we have to get out there and save the day. In fact, no one is asking us to be heroes.

White people are NOT *white saviors.* No Black or Indigenous person or any other person of the Global Majority I know has ever asked to be saved, and certainly not by this white boy.

Remember that whole thing about how language affects attitude and attitude affects behavior?

They have it so bad, somebody needs to do something about it— maybe it's me? he says, puffing out his chest, taking a wide stance, and thrusting his fists to his hips like Superman.

Um, not quite.

There are far more people in the world who are *not* white than are white. People of the Global Majority, people who do not identify as white, constitute over 80 percent of the world's population, and they are definitely not asking white people, a mere 20 percent of the population, to *save* them. It's not even about "people having it bad." It's about people who have rigged a system, and it's about that system that is *still* rigged to benefit white people. *That's* where our focus should be. *That's* what we need to work against.

But since I'm actually one of the people the system has been rigged to benefit, maybe, if I do want to combat that system, I need to first learn a lot more (A LOT more!) from the people who have been combating it for a long, long time.

There's a phrase I've heard people say that I like a lot and that works here: "There's a time for stepping up, and there's a time for stepping back." In other words, sometimes it's a great idea to stop standing by silently and get up and go DO something, but other times it's best to pause, look around, listen, and learn—because often there are already people DOING things, saying things, leading the fight against injustice, and it's best for us to listen to them first. And very often those leaders already leading are Black or Indigenous people or many other people of the Global Majority.

So right now—even though we're (hopefully, yeah?) all fired up to do something—we still need to step back.

I know. Annoying. Especially after I just finished saying we need to step *up*.

And I *am* saying white people need to step up and do something, yes, *and* . . .

We *can* do something by *listening*. Listening more often and listening more closely—especially to Black and Indigenous people, and all people of the Global Majority.

Uh, you want us to sit around and listen? That sounds so boring.
Sure, it's not hitting the three-pointer while falling

out-of-bounds when your team's down by two with only two seconds to go, but no team can win a whole season of games if that's all they're relying on. They probably can't win that many games at all, actually, if that's the big plan. In fact, that's a bad bet. But what *does* make a team win a whole season of games—that's right, no surprise here—is *teamwork*. And all teamwork relies on—that's right, you guessed it again—really good listening.

In the same way, in order for white people to better understand and learn about racism in America, we need to be better listeners. Honestly, I think white people like me just have not done a great job listening to people who are not white in America—even when we think we are.

Like that time my friend and I messed up big-time in Albuquerque, New Mexico.

Messing Up

When I was a teacher, my school administration enthusiastically encouraged and funded faculty and staff to attend workshops and seminars to help us expand our racial consciousness. I was super psyched about this. I brought my whiteness into the classroom every day, and this had an effect on my teaching for all my students, regardless of their racial identity. I just knew it. So I wanted to be as aware of it as I could, and when I heard that a few of my educator friends were going to the White Privilege Conference, I could hardly sign up fast enough.

While at the conference I attended a workshop in which

the facilitators had a mock race around a track. They solicited volunteers from the crowd, asking for a few people who identified as Latinx, and a few who identified as Asian American, and a few who identified as Black, and a few who identified as white. The idea was that, at first, those who volunteered to be in this race would all begin on the starting line together.

But then the facilitators asked the participants to take two steps forward if they were white.

And another two steps forward if they were debt-free and had graduated from college.

And two more steps forward if they identified as male.

I mean, just seeing that image so stark and clear at the front of the room—the size of those leads the white men up front—it kind of blew my mind. There was nothing "equal" about this race at all.

The process of visually spreading the pack of volunteers and giving certain people "leads" before the race even began was a brilliant way to make privilege more visible and drive home what it meant. In literally five minutes notions that all people have an equal shot in America (or "start in the same place" to begin the race) were torn to shreds. So white men were way out front, and the workshop also included "starting points" for Latinx people, Black people, people of Asian descent; it made adjustments for gender and sexuality, because they, too, play a role in giving people advantages on the "racetrack" for professional status and economic wealth in America.

The facilitators were about to move on to their next exercise when a Native American woman in the audience stood up. She wanted to know why the racetrack model, why the entire workshop, did not include or allude to, in any way, Indigenous people in the United States. *"This,"* she went on to explain, "is the kind of erasure we face every day."

She wasn't loud. Her voice didn't boom or fill the room. Rather, she was soft-spoken, as if pulling us all closer to her, as if making the huge hotel ballroom so much smaller— so much more intimate. The effect was that the people the facilitators had forgotten, had erased, were right there in the middle of all of us in the room.

She stood. She spoke. She would not be ignored.

I was floored. Because at a workshop at an anti-racist con- ference *an entire people*—all Indigenous cultures—was left out of the discussion. I know the woman stated her tribal affiliations at the time, and it embarrasses me to admit that I cannot recall them now. When she interrupted the workshop, I felt an agita- tion buzz through me, the kind I might get from my own stage fright or nervousness when standing in front of a crowd.

It was bad. Not because she stood up and interrupted the workshop and REMAINED STANDING FOR THE REST OF THE WORKSHOP SO THAT SHE WOULD BE SEEN AND NOT FORGOTTEN. It was bad because the facilitators had forgotten her, had erased her, and had erased all Indigenous people in America from the "anti-racist exercise" in their workshop. And I think part of the gut-clenching shame I felt was from having to have the woman point this out to *me* as much as she did the facilitators. If she hadn't stood and said something, I would have walked away from the workshop not even realizing that Indigenous people had been left out. Forgotten. Erased.

Even *more* troubling? The conference was being held in Albuquerque, New Mexico, and part of the focus of the conference was to *acknowledge local Indigenous culture*. To make *sure* the experience of Indigenous people was included in our discussions about white privilege at the conference. On top of *that*, each of the three days of the conference began with a welcome ceremony and smudging from one of the many Navajo, Apache, and Pueblo Nations in New Mexico.

And yet. Unbelievably (though for many Indigenous people, maybe far *too* believably), the facilitators that morning had left Indigenous people out. Native people had no starting point on the racetrack—until she stood. Until she spoke up.

The facilitators felt embarrassed. They tucked their chins to their chests. Mumbled their apologies and acknowledged their mistakes.

I felt ashamed.

And I wanted to get rid of that feeling of shame as fast as possible—tip the shame/pride scale back to feeling more confident than uneasy. Nobody *likes* to feel ashamed. But . . .

Sometimes we just have to sit with it. Sometimes by sitting with it, we learn a little more. We change a little bit. We grow.

The air in the workshop room drew tight. White people in the room, and especially the workshop facilitators, who, as I recall, were all white, fell silent with shame. A friend, a white woman, leaned close and whispered to me that she wanted to say something. She wanted to act. Do something. Show the Native American woman that she was willing to do something publicly in solidarity. Let the workshop leaders know that they'd caused immeasurable harm and that she was going to walk out of the workshop in protest.

She asked me if I'd join her.

Now, making a protest out of the moment was not what I wanted to do. To be honest, I felt in my gut there was something performative (*Hey, look at me! Look what I'm doing here!*) about standing up and declaring a protest in that moment. After all, *we* hadn't noticed the omission either! But, like I said, I felt ashamed and wanted to get the heck rid of that feeling, and this was a plan. It was something we could DO, right? And by DOING something, we'd get rid of the shame, right? And people would think, what? That we were "good" white people—even though we hadn't been aware of the erasure either until the woman stood?

Right?

Wrong.

Come on, Brendan. So very, very wrong.

So my friend stood and declared her intention, and I did the same, and we were both about to storm out of the workshop, arms swinging like we were marching in a parade—until the Native American woman turned back around to us.

"No," she implored. "Don't go. That's what you always do. You can always walk away. Stay here. Sit with this."

And she was as 1,000 percent right as I was 1,000 percent wrong.

Walking away, not engaging with the difficulty of the

moment, was what living as a white person often allowed me to do. I was uncomfortable, but I had an out—I could leave. Frankly, that was right in line with what I'd been taught to do—*don't talk about race*. We could declare an act of protest and feel good about ourselves and leave. *That* wasn't listening to what the woman had to say. *That* wasn't sitting with how it felt to know that, had we been the facilitators, we'd have done the exact same thing, and so, just like them, we would have hurt this woman by excluding her from the workshop. That *wasn't* taking responsibility.

That was running away. *That* was not listening. *That* was not dealing with what it means to recognize you are one of the people who can and does cause pain. *That* was saying, *It's your problem, not mine. You deal with it,* instead of owning up to the fact that it was actually our problem as much as it was the facilitators'.

Ooof. So much for *doing something*.

But wait. We *could* actually do something. In fact, the woman went on to explain what we could do that would be helpful.

Instead of running away, she asked us to actually sit in the room and participate in trying to figure out a way to proceed, or at the very least to just listen to what she and the other Indigenous people in the room had to say.

"Don't walk away," she repeated. "That's what you always do, walk away." She went on, "Please. Stay."

That was *doing something*.

Staying.

Listening.

I could witness the erasure of Indigenous people right then, so that going forward, I could try to lessen and decrease the erasure of Indigenous people by standing with them and not walking away.

She challenged our privilege and asked us to take some responsibility for it. To let the erasure sink in.

"Erasure" isn't just a fancy, intellectual word. It isn't just an idea. It causes bone-deep pain and harm.

So if we had walked, we would have walked away from her pain. We would have protected ourselves from feeling any of it as well. Even in our righteousness, we would have been compounding and adding to her pain.

But we were protesting!

No. We were adding to the pain.

And, yes, even at an anti-racist white privilege conference, white people were continuing to cause harm.

Whenever I have the urge to think of myself as "woke," I think of that moment. I think of the woman asking us to bear witness. There is no end to the amount of time I still need to bear witness, to listen, to learn, to try to feel more, to try to figure out the responsible thing to do—not just *show* that I'm doing *some*thing, regardless of what that "thing" is. Part of being privileged is to be ignorant, and therefore, part of what white people like me need to remember is how much work we still need to do (every day) to continue to learn more about *what we don't know.*

It's why, more than anything else we can do right now, we need to—we must—listen to the people who know a lot more than us and who have been leading this fight against racism for a long time, or surviving this racism for a long time.

It's one of the reasons I will never identify myself as "woke." I still have waaaaay too much "waking" to do.

16

Messing Up . . . and Listening

Soooo, Chapter 15 was getting a little long, so this really is just 15 extended . . . more on how it all comes back to listening.

All right. All right. More about listening. I know, I know. But to spark it up a bit, I'm bringing in professional basketball star Kyle Korver to help me make the point I'm trying to make: *becoming better listeners is absolutely key to us better understanding our white privilege and how to take some responsibility for racism and white privilege.* (Whew, that was a mouthful, but it really is what I'm getting at.)

Kyle Korver (who's played for a number of teams, set an NBA record for highest three-point shooting accuracy, played in two NBA Championships with the Cleveland Cavaliers, and most recently played with the Milwaukee Bucks) has a lot to say about white privilege. And accountability.

Kyle Korver is white. One night before a game in New York City, his teammate Thabo Sefolosha, a Black man, was out at a club. But the fun didn't last long because by the end of the night he had gotten into a scuffle with the police and gotten his leg broken. When Kyle learned about that night, about the differences between how he experienced life as an NBA player and how too many Black players and all players of the Global Majority experienced life as they traveled around the country, he began thinking about how unlikely it would have been for him to have his own leg broken by police in the same situation. And that led him to think about his privilege. And *that* got him thinking about his responsibility to do something to combat racism.

He decided it was about time that he held himself accountable.

Here's what he said:

> Two concepts that I've been thinking about a lot lately are *guilt* and *responsibility*.
> When it comes to racism in America, I think that guilt and responsibility tend to be seen as more or less the same thing. But I'm beginning to understand how there's a real difference.

As white people, are we *guilty* of the sins of our forefathers? No, I don't think so.

But are we *responsible* for them? Yes, I believe we are.

And I guess I've come to realize that when we talk about solutions to systemic racism—police reform, workplace diversity, affirmative action, better access to healthcare, even reparations? It's not about guilt. It's not about pointing fingers, or passing blame.

It's about responsibility.

Kyle Korver didn't always think this way. At first when he heard about what had happened to his teammate, he asked why Thabo Sefolosha was going out to a club the night before a game in the first place. He wondered what Thabo might have done to cause the police to drag him around and eventually (by accident, he assumed) break Thabo's leg. In fact, he even admits it: "Before I knew the full story, and before I even had the chance to talk to Thabo . . . I sort of *blamed* Thabo." Kyle basically assumed that if he (Kyle Korver) had been in the club, the police wouldn't have arrested him because he wouldn't have been doing anything wrong—and he therefore just assumed Thabo must have done something wrong.

Time passed all the way into the next season, until a racially charged incident during a game changed the way Kyle thought about race and racism and white privilege in particular. A white fan started calling a Black basketball player, Russell Westbrook, all kinds of racial slurs. After the game

Kyle sat in a closed-door meeting with his entire team, and he listened to all the players who were Black or other people of the Global Majority talk about similar incidents they'd had. And it was sitting there in the room, not walking away, not making any more assumptions, that Kyle started to realize just how different his experience as a professional basketball player was *because he was white*.

The more he thought about it, the more he thought about how privileged his life in the NBA was compared to his Black teammates and all the players of the Global Majority in the league. He cared about racial justice, he thought (and he did!), but he realized that even his caring about racial justice was a choice to *opt in* to care—it was a *privilege* for him to have a choice to care.

Because he was white.

Similar to what I realized when I was running around with my friends in the dark as a kid—that even though I wasn't the one holding the TV remote, even though I wasn't the one who nearly gave an old woman a heart attack, I still had to take some responsibility for the actions and behaviors of the group I was a part of—Kyle Korver also realized the very fact that he was white meant he had to take some responsibility for the racism and racial injustice in our country. The racist comments from fans were bad, but he now recognized that the violence his teammate Thabo Sefolosha suffered at the hands of police the year before was so much worse and absolutely connected to the kind of racist slurs his colleagues of color heard all the time in their life in the NBA and were telling him about that very minute.

Kyle realized how wrong his thinking had been back when Thabo had been hurt. How many times had he been wrong in the past, times when he'd made assumptions about other people without thinking about his own white privilege?

So, if he claimed to care (and he did!), he needed to learn more. He needed to listen more to the people who knew more than him—in particular, to Black and Indigenous people, and anyone of the Global Majority.

He said:

> The fact that Black Americans are more than five times as likely to be incarcerated as white Americans is *wrong*. The fact that Black Americans are more than twice as likely to live in poverty as white Americans is *wrong*. The fact that Black unemployment rates nationally are double that of overall unemployment rates is *wrong*. The fact that Black imprisonment rates for drug charges are almost six times higher nationally than white imprisonment rates for drug charges is *wrong*. The fact that Black Americans own approximately one-tenth of the wealth that white Americans own is *wrong*.
>
> The fact that inequality is built so deeply into so many of our most trusted institutions is *wrong*.
>
> And I believe it's the responsibility of

anyone on the privileged end of those
inequalities to help make things right.

The emphasis is his, not mine, and he finishes his piece
with these two lines:

Thanks for reading. Time for me to shut up
and listen.

Who?

I've got to say: Kyle Korver's advice just makes me pause a second. Makes me wonder. Who in my life do I need to listen to more?

Have you ever wondered about that? Who in your life you could listen to more?

Really listen to?

18

Listening . . . without Getting Defensive

"Listening? That's all I do all day," I've heard some people whine. "I mean, haven't we heard enough about race and racism and all that?"

Actually, no. Because I don't think white people like me *have* been listening. Maybe we've been *hearing*, but there's a big difference between *hearing* and really *listening*.

You can hear the bell at the end of the school day . . . or you can listen to it, know that its sound announces so much more, means so much more—it means out the door and over to so-and-so's place to get back to the Mario Kart tournament! Or whatever you want to do after school.

You don't just hear it. You listen. It's not just sound. It has meaning.

Maybe another way of thinking about it is that hearing is sensory recognition. It's like, *Oh, yeah, I hear that person speaking to me. Those are words. I recognize them.* But listening is taking it in, considering the sounds and what they mean. *Oh, that person is telling me about why they feel so afraid—they are afraid. Wow, I should check in on them. See if there's anything I can do to help.*

When someone shares things with you that make them super excited or nervous or gutted or teary-eyed or fist-clenching mad, they are opening the door to their heart to you. They've invited you in. You are their guest in the hallway of their heart. When invited, let's always be respectful guests.

We can listen.

Have you ever had a conversation with someone that was so infuriating because even though you were both speaking the same language, you weren't *speaking the same language*?

Like this:

Person 1: You know what? This COVID thing makes me so scared. I'm so scared to leave my house. I'm scared to look at the mail.

Person 2: Yeah, it's crazy, right? But you shouldn't be scared, because as long as you protect yourself, you'll be fine.

Person 1: No, I know. But I'm telling you, I'm scared.

Person 2: Seriously, you shouldn't be scared. It's important to keep a clear head and not let your fears run away from you.

Person 1: But I'm telling you—

Person 2: I'm telling *you*! Don't be scared.

Person 1: (Looks away at the floor.)

Person 2: Okay?

Person 1: (Still looking at the floor.)

Person 2: Are you okay? What's the matter?

Person 1: (Looks up, pissed!) I'm scared, I told you!

Person 2: Well, you actually sound mad to me.

Person 1: (Walks away.)

Person 2: (Shouting at Person 1's back:) It's not my fault you're scared. Don't be mad at me!

So, a couple words about Person 2. Person 2, why are you such a jerk? What's the matter with you? How about when a person says they're scared, you start by asking them to explain more or, depending on how well you know them, ask them if they need a hug. Why not LISTEN to what Person 1 is saying, rather than hearing their words as a tee up to debate?

I think about conversations like this all the time when I think about how white people often enter conversations about race. We're not really listening to people of the Global Majority, and so we say things that sound like, "Hey, yeah, so, no, I already know what you're saying, but have you thought about it this way?" or worse, "Hey, no, so, I know more than you do."

Well, we don't.

I know I don't!

There have been many, many times I have been in a group of people and witnessed white people stumbling over the names of people of East Asian, South Asian, African, or Arabic descent. Now, it is also true that people mispronounce my last name all the time. And in the past I remember trying so hard to be "in the know," trying so hard to buddy up to a person of the Global Majority by saying, "Yeah! Me too! People mess up my name all the time."

Even if I was "coming from a good place"—ever hear that expression?—with that comment, I'm still not doing a good job listening. First things first, I myself could work a little harder to try to get it right. But secondly, breezily saying, "Yeah, me too!" is more than just insensitive. Names are powerful—they are a gateway to getting to know someone or for someone to get to know you. There's a lot of research that shows that white people who review resumes for job openings are more likely to grant interviews to people with familiar-looking names (i.e., other white people). And that Black and Asian people, in particular, who "whiten" their resumes by "masking" their race have better success at landing job interviews.

I mean, come on! Of course I'm more likely to get a job if the person sifting through resumes calls me first only because of *how my name is pronounced*!

And it's not just about jobs. More times than I can count, I have been in a room with white teachers and administrators at schools who have made comments like, "Whatever happened to people with names like Mary and Joe?"

Oh, and guess what? Yup. I have a Mary *and* a Joe in my white family.

So when people of various racial and ethnic backgrounds who often get discriminated against talk about that discrimination and I say, "Yeah, me too," I'm not really listening. In fact, I glided right past their emotions, and I'm asking them to talk about me and *my* trouble with my name instead! How insensitive is that?

Most people don't want to be insensitive. And we try not to be. And . . . you might be one of those white (gulp) "woke" people who already knows all about white privilege. Who knows how deep and wide racism runs. Knows we must strive to fight against it. I am suuuuurely a white person like that too, but I'm constantly shocked at how often I forget that

that doesn't exempt me from *being white*. I'm not an exceptional white person—I'm just yet another white person, living my white life. All white people are.

Because even if I think of myself as a white person who is "sensitive to" or "aware of" issues of race and racism, if I don't really listen when Black and Indigenous people and all people of the Global Majority are telling me how race and racism affect their lives, or about how they see my white privilege affecting my life, then I'm not really the kind of "sensitive" white person *I thought* I was at all, am I?

One night in college I sat in the large common area in one of the dorms. The room was packed with white students listening to a handful of Black students tell us about their experience being Black at Miami University. (In 2019 there were 17,246 students enrolled at the Oxford, Ohio, campus, and only 615 of them identified as Black; from 1995 to 1999, when I attended, the proportion of Black students at Miami was likely very much the same.) Although I felt bad about what they were saying, I also felt the need to defend myself. I didn't say it out loud, but on the inside I was shouting, *But not me! Not me! Not me! I don't do that.* So while I was listening to them (or supposed to be listening to them) talk about what *they* had to deal with, all I *wanted* to hear was one of them say, *That's how many white people here make us feel, but not you, of course. You are an exception to that.*

Maybe there is something natural about wanting to hear about yourself in some exceptional way. But not entirely. How much of my ego in that moment was based on what I assumed or imagined was hurtful white-people behavior instead of what the Black students were *actually saying* was hurtful white-people behavior?

My throat runs dry just remembering the way my eyes darted around the room, the way they fell to the floor in front of me when any one of them looked at me as they shared their stories, the overwhelming silence (not from listening—that's different) I offered in return for their courage and strength to share their stories. How could I have been anything but yet another one of those white faces who stared at them through sideways glances and made them feel uncomfortable, unwelcome? Why couldn't I have found some courage to speak up and say, *I believe you,* to say, *I'm sorry when I am one of those people, and I'd like to do better?*

That would've been a pretty low bar to meet in order for me to be a decent human being. But I didn't even meet that bar that day.

So here's the thing: when someone is sharing their pain, their anger, their sadness, listen with interest and courage.

Here is *not* the thing: don't get defensive, need to feel like the exception, need to feel like the "good" white person as opposed to all those "other" white people. Don't condescend ("No, I know this already") or belittle ("No, but let me tell you how it really is")—those are definitely *not* the thing either. In fact, they can be really hurtful.

This is hard—I get that. I really do. It's so easy to say, "But look at all the progress that has been made." That's a whole lot easier than actually listening to the pain Black and Indigenous people and so many people of the Global Majority are talking about *right now*. Because when we listen to their pain, we as white people are part of the cause of it, and we can't blame it on the slaveholders of previous centuries, or the racist governors and sheriffs of the 1950s and '60s, or our sad uncle who always wants to sneak in that joke he knows he'll be told not to finish but thinks is funny anyway. This is why it is so important for all of us, white people included, to talk about—and listen about—racism and white privilege when we are with our families, in our religious and spiritual congregations, in our schools and libraries, and in our civic communities.

Because the pain isn't only yesterday. It's today. It's right now.

And we helped cause it—today—and that's hard to hear.

But we can't run away from the uncomfortableness we feel when we hear about the pain of others or the pain we ourselves have caused. We shouldn't protect ourselves from it or try to distance ourselves from it. We should sit with it, just as the woman in Albuquerque told me, in order to grow and learn and not repeat the mistakes of our past.

Like this other time I messed up in college.

Back then I was that floppy-haired guy who looked way too much like Shaggy from the Scooby-Doo cartoons. I walked like him. Flap, flap, flap went my big feet beneath my lanky legs. I talked like him. My voice dipped up and down in a weird warble-squeak. My clothes didn't fit me right—well, it was the 1990s, when many of us were lost in clothes that were too baggy. But most importantly, I spoke with a loose kind of slang, addressing people as "dude" or "man," as in, "Hey, man," or "brother," like "What's up, brother?"

And I didn't think much of it until a friend came by my dorm room and I gave him one of those greetings. "What's up, brother? Come on in."

Now, though this was a friend, I'd never called him that before. Not for any reason. I just hadn't used that part of my (limited) lexicon with him before. But out it popped this time, and I was all smiles and waving him in to hang out, and he cocked his head back and stared at me.

"Brother?"

His face twisted in confusion.

This friend? He's Black.

Just a reminder: I'm white.

"What'd you say?"

"Oh, no. No. I'm sorry. I didn't mean it like that."

"Yeah. Don't do that."

I was in no way trying to say something funny or offensive or be anything other than friendly, but when I said it, I rubbed him the wrong way, and I offended him. In some cases, or with some people, this might not have been a problem. But at that moment it was. He'd certainly never called me "brother" before. I'm not stating some kind of rule about whether or not a white guy calling a Black guy "brother" is right or wrong. People in their own authentic relationships are going to make up their own rules.

My focus here is my whiteness. In particular, though I meant no offense, what was the point of me trying to explain to him that I'd meant no offense? What was the goal? For him to eventually tell me, *It's okay. You're a good person?* Was I really trying to guilt-trip him into saying, *Never mind, I was wrong to be offended?* Was I really trying to twist it around so that *he* had to make *me* feel better?

HE JUST TOLD ME that I had offended him.

So guess what? I *had* offended him. Full stop.

I don't need to get defensive when someone does that. Instead . . .

I can just listen. Get out of my own way and listen.

Listen. And trust that what I'm hearing is true.

Listen. And own it, Brendan.

And try, as hard as I can, not to make that mistake again.

19

Listening . . . and Believing

You ever listen to a song over and over until you know the lyrics by heart, and then, when you get to certain lines or some particular point in the song, you actually feel something in your body? Like your throat clenches just a bit, the way it does when it runs dry, when you want to hold back a tear. And it starts to feel like the singer is right there, over your shoulder, watching what happened to you, and is now singing about you, is telling you, *See, you are not alone . . . see, I saw that too . . . see, what you are* *feeling right now, right now, that is real and I feel it too, and feeling it together means neither of us has to feel alone.*

You know what I mean?

This could be anybody's song. Lizzo, The Weeknd, Taylor Swift—whoever's song it is that cocoons you deep inside your feelings. A song your gospel choir sings. Something you learned at summer camp. That song you always hear your friends playing but don't know the name of, even though you know all the words.

Whatever. You get my point. Some song you absolutely love because it makes your soul hum.

I love music. I listen to music when I write. I listen to music when I work out. I listen to music when I'm walking to the grocery store. I listen to music when I'm on the subway. I listen to music when I'm driving, when I'm cooking dinner, when I'm doing laundry, when I'm hanging out with friends, when I'm cleaning the damn bathroom.

I listen to music that makes my soul hum.

And even though it's music, what I'm getting at is that it makes my soul hum because I'm open to it. I'm actually *ready* to be moved by it. I *want* to be moved by it.

So here's a wild idea: What if we listened to each other like that? What if we listened to our friends like that? What if we listened to people who were telling us an important story about their life like that?

Open. Ready to be moved. Ready to be changed.

That is some kind of better listening.

I met a student in Maine, a high school student who asked

me one of the most difficult questions I've ever been asked. I think she was getting at this idea of better listening in her question, which was this:

> "Do you think white people will finally empathize with the pain of racism when they become a majority minority in schools all across America?"

So, I'd been speaking to the school about my books, about racism, about white privilege, and we'd just been talking about the fact that there will be more students of the Global Majority than white students in K–12 public schools in America by the year 2023. Meaning that for the first time since public schools were created in the United States, students of the Global Majority, including Black, Indigenous, Latinx, and Asian students, will be the majority. Therefore, white kids will be the majority minority.

Now, this particular student was a young Black woman in a school where overwhelmingly, the majority was white, which is an incredibly important fact in this context. The questions that usually come up in the discussions I have in schools might be inspired by pride, excitement, fear, curiosity, pain, mean-spiritedness, joy—any powerful emotion that can take hold of a person. I don't know what inspired this student's question, but I do know that it took an enormous amount of courage to ask it.

And, as a white person, it was gut-wrenching trying to answer it.

Empathy. There might be plenty of white people who say they feel bad that racism exists. There might be plenty of white people who say they feel bad *for* people who suffer the pain of racism, the disadvantages of racism, the bullying of racism. But empathy isn't feeling something *for* someone. Empathy is more feeling something *with* someone. Say you're watching someone get bullied. Feeling bad for the kid getting bullied is not empathy. But actually feeling *as if you yourself* were the one getting bullied? That's empathy.

So that's what the first part of her question was about: *Will white people finally empathize with the pain of racism?*

It's the second part that was the real dig. She was asking if white people will feel the pain ourselves only once we are no longer the majority. Put another way, what she was asking, I think, is if white people will finally "get" the pain when we're the marginalized group ourselves—is that what it would take, being bullied ourselves, to finally feel *with* the kids (not just for the kids) who've been racially bullied all along? Is that where we'd find our empathy?

Her question turned me inside out. I'm still trying to figure out how to answer it.

Because, hey, real talk: it's not empathy if we have to actually live it to feel it.

"Empathy" is a tricky word and a complicated concept. Sometimes we think we feel *with* someone, and sometimes, because we *think* we do, we then think we *know* or *understand* what it feels like to be that other person. And that, to me, is crossing a line. That's beyond feeling with—that's saying (remember from the last chapter?), "No, I know. I *know exactly* what you mean."

Here's an example:

When I was in high school, I was very interested in trying to help the homeless. My school required us to do sixty hours of community service as a condition for graduating. I chose to help prepare food in my school's kitchen, which we then took to a homeless shelter, where we finished preparing and serving the meal.

Then one day I explained to my father, "Hey, Dad, this is what I'm going to do. I'm going to go out and be homeless for a couple of nights, and then I'm going to come back home, but because I'll have been homeless for a couple of nights, I'll have a better understanding of what it means to be homeless."

My dad's response? He just shook his head and said, "Brendan, listen to yourself. Listen to what you just said. You're going to go be homeless and then come *home*? You have no idea what it means to be homeless. You can't just pretend to be homeless for a couple of days. That's like you saying you'll be Black for a couple of days to understand what it means to be Black. You can never understand," he told me, "what it means to be a Black man in America. Don't pretend."

Well, that sure woke me up! I just stood there, blinking, taking all that in.

Taking that in . . . We are who we are. We can never *really* be the other people we say we care about and want to help. We can never really be anyone other than who we are. We can *try* to empathize with others, but we can't wholly understand an experience we haven't lived. I can't pretend I *know* someone else's life—and so maybe instead, I should just try harder to listen to them telling their own story.

And then . . . wait for it . . . just *believe* them.

I think this idea approaches what the student in Maine was getting at as well: *When will you just believe me, believe what I'm saying? What will it take?*

Why do I need to see something or feel something before I believe it? Why can't I just believe the personal stories of people who have been telling me about the effects of racism on their lives for so long? How hard is that?

How exhausting and endlessly frustrating it must be to tell the same stories of racism and cultural bullying and personal pain—for decades, for centuries—and not be believed! Can you imagine if you told people about something awful that happened to you and nobody believed you? Or maybe one group believed you but another didn't?

That's exactly what it's been like, what it is like, for all too many people who are not white in America. Because collectively, over time, too many of us white people (even when we don't mean to at all) have been gaslighting people of the Global Majority instead of at least trying to empathize or believe them when they share their stories of individual or group pain.

What's "gaslighting"? It's an emotional manipulation

strategy meant to screw with someone's mind.

Basically, it works like this:

Person A tells Person B, "Hey, this happened to me."

Person B says, "Oh, no, you don't understand. You have it all wrong."

And even though Person A is telling the truth, Person B makes Person A doubt *their own truth*. That's messed up, right? In fact, the medical profession calls gaslighting a "form of psychological abuse."

And how does this relate to racism? Well, when conversations about racism come up, how many times have you heard a white person say something like: "Nah, but it isn't *that* bad anymore . . ." or "Yeah but, that's the past . . ." or "But, come on, we've had a Black president now, so . . ." or "Look at all the *progress* that's been made . . ."

That last line is uncomfortably familiar to me because I've said it myself. I even remember saying it to a Black woman once—at the time I thought the way I said it also implied, *And isn't that a good thing?* The conversation began with her telling me how she'd felt iced out of a job opportunity, then it morphed into a larger discussion about systemic racism, and by the time I blurted my line about "progress," even though I thought we were having an abstract, intellectual conversation about job opportunity, she was still speaking about getting passed over for a job she knew she was qualified for and for which she knew her being Black played a role in getting passed up.

What I didn't understand was that when I said, "Look at all the progress that's been made," what it sounded like to her—a person who was telling me the truth about having been personally affected by a very hurtful experience of racism—was, *Get over it* or *You're making a mountain out of a mole-hill* or *Yeah, but that's just one interaction; in the big picture it's better than that.* In other words, I was gaslighting. I was dismissing her truth, saying something to make her dismiss her truth.

(Quick aside: The conversation ended when she told me I needed to get more educated because I didn't know what I was talking about, and I realized with a jolt of self-disgust how much I'd hurt her . . . and more educated, I very much wanted to get.)

Another thing I didn't know at the time of that conversation was how often white people say things like that. How often we say things about racism thinking we are "factually correct," when *in fact*:

(a) We might not be, but we still speak with an authoritative tone, *as if* we are factually correct.

And even more important:

(b) The subtext of whatever we're saying sounds like, *I don't believe you* or *You have to say more, show me more, prove to me more, in order for me to believe you.*

This constant gaslighting, this constant demand for people of the Global Majority to have to "prove" how bad the racism they experience is, it only adds to and compounds the pain of that racism. Actually, I think part of what is so painful about racism in America is that the burden to prove, to show, to reveal the horrors of racism falls again and again on the people of the Global Majority—when that shouldn't be the case!

That's what I think the girl in Maine was implying too. If

white people tried to empathize more with the people of the Global Majority when they're sharing their experiences with racism, if more of us chose to believe in the magnitude and overall pervasiveness of the monstrosities of racism, then we might more readily jump in to do our part to acknowledge, reveal, and expose how often racism affects people's lives.

This, I think, is one of the reasons why a woman you may or may not have heard of, by the name of Mamie Till-Mobley, was so courageous and monumental in the civil rights movement in the late 1950s: she was determined to make sure white people would see, witness, and therefore *have to believe* her story about the horror and pain of racism.

Her son, Emmett Till, was a fourteen-year-old Black boy who was brutally murdered by two white men in 1955. Emmett was on his summer vacation, visiting relatives in Mississippi, when the white men came to his uncle's house, kidnapped Emmett, beat him, mutilated him, shot him in the head, and then dumped his body in the Tallahatchie River. They were seeking revenge, claiming Emmett had flirted with the wife of one of the men.

In and of itself, this was barbarity of the highest order. But then, as if all that weren't terrible enough, an all-white jury found the white men *not guilty* of kidnapping or murder. They were sent home *free*. The following year, in a magazine interview, the men even admitted to killing Emmett! But by law, a person cannot be charged with the same crime twice. Therefore, these murderers lived the rest of their lives free.

Now, remember how, after George Floyd was murdered, my friend had to tell his son that often the people who commit violence—when they are white and the violence is against Black and Indigenous people, and so many different people of the Global Majority—go free?

I ask you to remember because, believe it or not, Emmett Till's story gets even worse.

Years later, after the men murdered Emmett Till, after they all got sent home free, and after they admitted to killing the boy, the white woman who'd claimed Emmett had flirted with her in the first place also admitted that she had lied about that.

Before Mamie Till-Mobley—Emmett's grieving mother—learned anything about who went free and who hid behind lies, she made an incredibly courageous choice. When her son's body was brought back to her in Chicago (which she had to fight to make happen), she chose to hold an open-casket funeral for her boy because she did not want what happened to him to get diminished in any way. She didn't want people to have an excuse to *not believe* what had most certainly happened to her son. And in order to make *not believing* impossible, she made sure the entire world would see him.

By doing so, her choice—her declaration that she wanted the world to see what had happened—shamed and horrified enough white Americans that they began to demand some justice in the case. They wrote op-eds and letters to the editor in newspapers. They tried to apply pressure to the legal and social systems in Mississippi. They were motivated to join some civil rights protests. And another unexpected result of Mamie Till-Mobley's bravery was that in some ways she opened the door to more white Americans' sympathies toward the civil rights movement of the 1950s and '60s.

But why? *Why?* Why did it have to come to this? Why? Why? Why?

Why did it take the sharing of a parent's worst nightmare—and the photographed and televised reality of it—to wake white people up?

That's why the student's question in Maine struck me as so profound. How much more do we have to *see* (in order to believe) before we finally feel moved to actually *do* something about all this racism? Does the violence have to be so heinous, so atrocious, that we literally cannot bear it as human beings?

Because we already saw that kind of violence in 1955 against Emmett Till. Then (in *another* list that is seemingly never-ending):

- Again in the bombing of the 16th Street Baptist Church in Birmingham, Alabama, in 1963.

- And again when twelve-year-old Santos Rodriguez was shot by police while handcuffed in 1973 in Dallas.

- And again when Michael Donald was lynched in 1981 in Mobile, Alabama.

- And again at the mass shooting at Emanuel African

Methodist Episcopal Church in Charleston, South
Carolina, in 2015.

- And again in the 5,712 cases of missing and
  murdered Indigenous women and girls reported
  by the National Crime Information Center in 2016,
  when only 116 of those cases were logged into the
  Department of Justice database.

- And again in 2021, when eight people, five of them of
  Korean descent and one of Chinese descent, were shot
  and killed in three spas in the Atlanta metro area.

- And still again in the staggeringly high increase in
  hate crimes leveled against East Asian Americans
  in 2020 and 2021. More than 6,600 hate incidents
  related specifically to racist (and wildly incorrect)
  COVID-19 blame-gaming were reported in the year
  following the start of the pandemic—and nearly
  an entire third of those incidents were reported in
  March 2021 alone. That's nearly 2,200 incidents in
  only ONE MONTH! How many more people in these
  communities need to speak up about these incidents
  before we really hear them?

And what about all the names and incidents we *don't* know
about because they weren't highlighted in the news? We
don't see them or hear about them, but do we not *believe they
are happening*?

Now, maybe you, personally, didn't see any of this—you

probably weren't even alive for some of it—but white people have watched these atrocities happen again and again and again. And yet they keep happening. Because we haven't done enough to help change it. To stop it.

That is part of white privilege. Too many white people say, "Not my problem. Someone else will fix this this."

But who? Or, rather, which white people are joining all the people of the Global Majority who are currently trying to create the necessary change and who have been working to try to create the necessary change for years and years and years?

Because when the girl in Maine's question is *When will you empathize?*, and it implies *When will you believe me?*, the question underneath all that might be, *When will you act?*

Sometimes people hear a question like that as a "call-out," a "Hey, you are doing something wrong, here!" And yes. That might be part of it. But I also hear in that question a "call in," a bold and courageous invitation to be vulnerable with the person who has asked that question. And when I think about it like that, then I think the answer to the girl in Maine's question begins with listening. Because listening *is an act*. It's the most important action we can take, because it's vital and necessary that we listen first, take it all in, really hear it, and then do more.

In fact, that's what the Native American woman in Albuquerque was saying too, right? Stay here. Listen. Don't run away because it hurts to hear. Be strong enough to listen—so you can be strong enough to do something else when it is necessary.

That's the kind of person I'd like to be. Someone who is strong enough to listen when it counts, even if it hurts a little—so that I can be strong enough to act again, when I need to.

For example:

When I was a teacher, my school began a project to try to highlight how racism and white privilege affected a multiracial cross section of high school students in New York City. The plan was to make a documentary showcasing this in the students' lives—and how they felt as they learned about that racism and white privilege. The organizers also enlisted a multiracial group of teachers from around the city to help design an educational curriculum that would be paired with the film.

When the idea was pitched to me, it sounded great! What a powerful tool! What an honor to be part of the project! We were going to change lives!

Yeah, but no.

No, no. And no!

The project fell apart nearly as soon as it began.

In a nutshell:

The entire project had been conceived, designed, fundraised, and managed by a small circle of mostly white men. And no matter how good their intentions, this was a supposedly "anti-racist" project in which Black people and other people of the Global Majority again and again felt like their voices, vision, wisdom, and professional expertise were being ignored and sidelined. And every time they brought that up, the white leadership said, in so many words, "No, it *has* to be *this* way, because that's how it's already been designed."

The irony of this "anti-racist" project being racist in its creation and implementation was deeply harmful.

When I agreed to join the project, I was ignorant. Everything sounded great, but I hadn't asked any questions about how the project had been designed. However, Black, Latinx, and Asian American friends of mine who were invited to participate all arrived cautious and prepared for what now, with hindsight, seemed so inevitable. The project blew up in the first few days.

I didn't arrive with the foresight of my Black, Latinx, and Asian American friends, but when I began to witness what was happening, when I began to see the faces of worry and pain rise around the room, when I heard my friends and colleagues voicing their concerns, even though a hornets' nest buzzed in my brain, I began to speak up and ask questions. I began to echo their concerns. I recognized that if I was any kind of friend—never mind ally or co-conspirator or anti-racist—at the bare minimum if I claimed to be a *friend* to my *FRIENDS*, the very least I could do was stand with them publicly, echo and amplify their observations and analyses, and affirm the emotions ballooning everywhere throughout the room.

This was something, but again . . . it was still not enough.

The Black, Latinx, and Asian American educators were essentially saying, over and over, *This is racist, and here's why,* and I was essentially saying in response, *Yeah, what she said. Yeah, yeah, what she said!*

At a certain point one of my friends, an Afro-Latinx woman, looked around the room and tried to meet me (and a few other white people in the room who had been speaking up) in the eye. And she said something to the effect of "I need to know that you'll speak up about the racism I'm talking about now—even when I'm not here saying it. I need to be able to trust that you are going to say what I'm saying right now, even when I'm not in the room with you."

I heard her. I listened to what she was saying. And as I thought about her words, I felt they implied something else, too. I felt like she was also saying, *Because if I can't trust that you will speak up when I am not in the room, how can I trust what you are saying now?*

In that moment I nodded in agreement and mumbled some weakened form of "I will," but I was fortunate to be in another meeting, months later, with many of the same people who were in this room, in which I found my voice and could promise with the conviction I truly felt.

"I promise I will speak up when you are not in the room."

I'm not patting myself on the back there—it's the bare minimum I could do as a friend!

But also, it's how listening becomes the road to more action. Because actually, that documentary movie did get made. And you know what? It was great, especially the young people in it—it's called *I'm Not Racist . . . Am I?*—and while that part of the project worked out in the end, the question at the heart of this story remains: Are we white people listening, and if we are, what are we going to do about what we hear and learn?

Remember how Kyle Korver said white people can just opt out of this conversation anytime we want? It's also part of our privilege, however, that we *can opt in* on the conversation, that we can *choose* to try to do something about racial injustice. That's true.

But we have to make that choice. Once we've listened, once we've held those stories, those truths, close to our hearts— we have to opt in.

Especially when we are with other white people.

All of us who are white live with white privilege. There's no escaping that.

But it's how each of us lives with it as an individual that tells the world who we really are.

So maybe that's the ultimate question:

Who are you?

Remember how, early on, I said I want to do better? Be better? I mean, I just want to be my better self. That's all. I feel like we all want to strive to be our best selves. And like I said way back near the beginning of all this, one way to do that is to talk about our racial identities—I mean really talk about them—with other white people. That's what this whole other talk is—has been—about!

See, if we really *are* listening, then when we *do* speak up, we have to start by talking about our privilege, talking about our history with honesty. Then we can talk about our present with honesty, which means talking about racism honestly, which in turn means talking about white privilege honestly . . .

. . . and talking about white privilege honestly *with other white people.*

I mean, that's what *other talk* is all about. That's what it is. That's the talk we have to have with other white people.

So now we can speak up? you ask.

Oh, hell yes.

20

Taking Action

Have you ever felt scared to speak up? Put yourself out there when no one else does?

I have. Honestly, still to this day, when I have to get up in front of an audience, or even when I'm just sitting in a room full of friends or other people I know, and I realize, *Oh, damn, I'm going to have to confront that person and say something to challenge them,* I feel my body squeeze, my shoulders press closer to my neck. I feel my heart whacking away in my chest, when only moments before, I could have forgotten it was even there.

Yup. Speaking up can be seriously scary.

Part of what makes it hard is that speaking up often means

being honest, *getting real* about something the people you have to say something to don't want to be honest about—don't even want to look at, let alone talk about. It's easy to be open and honest with people who already agree with you; it's when we have to speak up and be open and honest with people who disagree with us that speaking up gets tough. But we still have to do it. We have to talk about white privilege and racism, especially with other white people.

And when telling that truth, sometimes we need to make other white people uncomfortable. To do *that*, sometimes we need to make *ourselves* uncomfortable first.

When I played high school basketball, we had three teams: freshman, junior varsity, and varsity. When I was a sophomore, I played on the JV team, and as often is the case, the JV team would play first and then sit in the stands and cheer on the varsity team's game, because that's the really important game for the school, it was more than implied.

I'll never forget one game in particular. We were playing an away game. We were playing a school that had mostly Black and Latinx students, and my school was nearly all white. In fact, my team was all white. The JV game that I played in, I think we lost. I actually don't even remember if we won or lost, but after we played, we were watching the varsity game in the stands—and they were certainly losing. It was a pretty important game, and so my school had set up a "fan van" and bus to drive a whole bunch of fans from our school to this school to watch and cheer us on.

As our varsity team of all-white players began losing to

the other team of nearly all Black and Latinx players, a chant started in the stands where fans from my school were sitting: "That's all right. That's okay. You're going to work for us someday. That's all right. That's okay. You're going to work for us someday."

I remember feeling awful. The chant's condescension and smug entitlement gripped me like a flu I couldn't shake—and it was a flu, it was a kind of sickness inside me, because that condescending attitude was coming from people at my school. It was my community feeling so grossly superior to another—and I whether I liked it or not, it was my community acting that way.

And again. It was my nearly all-white community saying that to a nearly all Black and Latinx community, and that stark racial disparity between our two communities added another layer of nastiness to the chant because it was therefore also pointedly racist.

Think about the audacity. Think about the entitlement. Think about the ignorance it takes to feel like it was okay to shout that chant. Not only were the words rude, harmful, and disrespectful, but also we were in the other team's house, in front of their families, and we still, as a community, felt entitled to chant this. I wasn't just embarrassed; I was mortified. In fact, even though I was still wearing my St. John's basketball jacket, I got up from where I was sitting with my teammates, walked to the other side of the basketball court, and sat in the stands with the other school's community, because I couldn't bear to be a part of my school's community.

I got dirty looks from my teammates. I saw people in the stands, people from my school, pointing at me. I knew I'd get teased later. But I also knew I couldn't sit there and do nothing. Doing nothing felt like doing something, actually—it felt like I was supporting the chant, or even chanting along with them. So I had to do something else.

So I took my little protest to the other side of the court and sat there for most of the rest of the game.

Now, that doesn't make me a hero. Definitely not. That doesn't make me anything other than a somewhat decent human being who felt the ugliness of that chant, making me sweat with anger.

But what I *didn't* do that day, what makes me *not* a hero, and what has bothered me ever since—for twenty years!—is that I didn't say anything to any of my teammates. I didn't say anything to any of the people in the stands. I didn't turn around and say, *Cut the sh-t!* I didn't ask a coach to step in. I didn't ask any of the adults in the crowd to step in.

No one did.

The chant went on until it died down. Then, later, it started up again.

I was across the court, shaking my head. But that's all I was doing—shaking my head.

What I should have done was stay on my own school's side of the gym and try to get my fellow students and their families and friends to understand how offensive their chant was. I should have tried to stop it.

Because that's what I really needed to do there. I can't escape who I am and where I come from, but maybe, by working to try to get the group I belong to, the culture I come from, to change and grow, I, too, as an individual, can change and grow.

In other words, so much of my white privilege comes in all these moments when other white people see me as just another white person. So if I care about racial justice, then it means I have to take opportunities to talk to other white people, even friends and family . . . maybe even *especially* friends and family . . . about racism. About their racism. If I'm really being honest about white privilege, what I'm saying is, I have to talk to them about *our* racism, as white people. That's just part of my taking some responsibility.

Remember how the cop looked at me with compassion and pity that night I was speeding down the highway? Remember how I felt safe with the Uber driver who brought a gun along for when he drove through Black neighborhoods? My white privilege protected me, supported me, in those situations and so many others—made other white people ready and willing to listen to me.

So part of my white privilege is that I have to use it to speak up to other white people.

I'm not saying I have to have a confrontational conversation with a man with a gun on the seat beside him. That's NOT AT ALL what I'm saying. But I can send an email to the white organizers of the book festival and suggest they provide transportation to and from the airport for the attending authors so that no one of the Global Majority, and particularly no women of the Global Majority, has to get into a car and be confronted with that situation. I'm not saying we're out here to *save* any of those other authors from him. I'm saying we can take the time to talk to other white people about things we white people might take for granted, like our safety.

This is my responsibility. And yours, fellow white people.

This is why, as a white person, I need to start having these conversations about white privilege and racism *all the time* with my white friends and family. We need to do it and do it and do it again. Practice makes habit. And the courage we practice today forms the bedrock of courage we will need for tomorrow.

Because there will be times when doing the right thing— standing up and speaking out—will take courage. A lot of courage. Because sometimes people don't want to listen. Sometimes people who have control and power in your community, and who could make things better for everyone by changing some of their policies, won't listen.

In those cases we need the courage it takes to help them understand.

When I think about courage these days, I think a lot about a group of students (and the teachers who supported them) who mounted a gutsy protest at a high school in Brooklyn. Jason and I were going to speak at an assembly about our cowritten novel. But when we arrived, we discovered that a large group of students and a handful of teachers had taken over the lobby and had blocked entry to and exit from the school. They'd taken over the lobby during lunch, exactly at a time when many of the students and teachers usually fanned out into the neighborhood to get food from their favorite storefronts and restaurants. The atmosphere was tense. The protestors were nervous. There was fear in their eyes—but there was also fiery determination.

They were taking a major risk.

When Jason and I got to the door, we asked what the protest was about, and the group sent out a student ambassador who read us their list of ten demands. They wanted a designated safe space in the school for students of the Global Majority to gather. They wanted changes made to their curriculum. They wanted the administration to deal with a handful of teachers these students felt did not support their voices and needs in the school.

When the student ambassador finished, she looked up at us. "If you agree with our demands and you want to stand with us and ask our administration to make these changes, you can come in and link arms with our group. If you don't agree, I'm sorry, but you can't come into our school."

The student ambassador was a young Black woman. She was nervous—we could see it in her eyes; we could see it in the way the paper shook in her hands. Heck, I was nervous too! I glanced into the lobby and recognized one of the teachers, a Black woman who'd been part of the anti-racist project at my former school that had fallen apart. I could see the nervousness in her eyes as well.

But I also knew her. Knew the depth of her fearlessness. Knew the distance she'd go for her students—because she cared. In my experience there are always a handful of teachers at every school who will go that extra mile (hell, that extra *marathon*) for their students—and there is never not a right time to shout out some love for the teachers like her all across this country.

But it was the student who was in charge at that moment.

She said something to the effect of, "The teachers we are most concerned with are right across the street." She pointed out the glass doors to them. She went on to say something like, "We're not letting them in, because even if they *say* they agree with these demands, we know they do not." She looked up at us again and repeated her earlier qualification: if we agreed with their demands, then we could enter the school.

Jason and I didn't need to discuss it. We knew exactly how we felt, and we joined the protestors in the lobby immediately. They squeezed us in, and we linked arms with other students. Students and teachers in the group were taking turns making short speeches, sharing stories. People were crying. Students of the Global Majority, teachers of the Global Majority. White students, white teachers. One white girl and one Black girl stood together on a bench in the lobby and held hands and rested their heads against each other as they cried, their cheeks glistening under the lobby's halogen lights.

We stood with them for two hours as they continued to share stories and argue with administrators who came to plead with them to move. We said nothing. It wasn't our place to say anything. But we joined their ranks and supported their cause with our presence.

Eventually, we left when the negotiations were none of our business, and the story continued. The protest may have ended that day, but the conversations with the administration continued for a long time after. They even carried over into the following school year. And though the students did not get all ten of their demands met, they got quite a few, and it made their action all the more important.

This wasn't teen angst. This wasn't teens "just acting wild." They weren't naïve.

This was a thoughtful, well-reasoned, well-organized protest rooted in real-life problems and concerns. And because they took this action, and did it so effectively, they made the people with power at the school *really listen* and actually make some real changes that would improve the lives of all the students in the school. When those administrators really listened, when they were forced to hold the protesting students' stories in their own hearts in a way they had not before, they were moved to make policy changes grounded in the students' requests.

Again, did the students who protested get everything they wanted? No. Not enough. But it's an important lesson to learn that sometimes you don't get the whole reward for the whole risk you take.

No matter what, what they did accomplish was a start, and it shows that you need to take a risk to start anything, or change will never happen.

You need to take risks to make any change happen at all.

As I've said, history does live in the present . . . and this history lives in our present too:

The spirit of the protest at that Brooklyn school pulsed within the vast network of abolitionist families who helped establish the Underground Railroad across the Ohio River Valley in the mid-1800s. It hummed and sang in the thousands and thousands of people marching in the first gay pride parades in Chicago, New York, Los Angeles, and San Francisco in 1970. It chanted in the Black Lives Matter rallies in Minneapolis, Minnesota, in 2020.

What a history to be a part of . . . what a future to be a part of . . .

And what a thing to learn: to know that you can build a bridge between yesterday's courage and tomorrow's with your own courage today.

When I think about courage, I also think of Yusuf, the eighth grader in Massachusetts. I hear him speaking up and reading the lines from the note tacked up to his mosque's door. I hear him speaking so that his truth would be heard.

Well, as I write these lines, Yusuf is now a senior in high school. And in the wake of the murder of George Floyd in 2020, Yusuf and a group of students organized a (virtual— this is also the year of the pandemic) community conversation. This group of students, mostly students of the Global Majority but also some white students, wanted their city in Massachusetts to discuss how and why the murder of George Floyd related to them. They wanted the community to show up to talk about racism and white privilege. Because *real conversation, real listening,* is important action, is something we *can* do—we might not be able to stop all police brutality across the country, but maybe, just maybe, we can at least minimize some of the impact of racism and white privilege in our own community . . . one conversation at a time. And that was what Yusuf and his friends set out to do. To stand up and speak up about racism and white privilege.

More than one hundred people showed up to participate in this community conversation—and to listen. Many, many of these people were white kids. White kids who were there to listen. White kids who were there to learn. White kids who were there to support the leadership of Yusuf and the other student leaders in their community.

Yusuf and his friends got the conversation started, but how might it grow? Who else is going to jump in where they left off and keep the conversation relevant, keep it moving, keep it shaking things up and inspiring more people in the community? Who are the white people who are going to speak up about white privilege in that community—or in yours?

When you stand up and speak out, you never know what effect you might have in your community. And you don't always get to see the results of your work, but it doesn't mean your work didn't pay off.

When I was in high school, there was a small group of us who wanted to start a club called TASC—The Association for Social Consciousness. We had big dreams. We wanted the school to place a greater priority on racial justice and feminism. Being at an all-boys, nearly all-white Catholic school, my friends and I worried that too many of our classmates cared too little. Even though there were teachers talking about racial justice and feminism, and even though there were powerful quotes about compassion and equality on the walls and in homilies we heard at Mass, too much of the attitude and atmosphere in the student body was still scarily racist and anti-women. So we met with the administration. And we worked hard trying to organize a week of awareness in which we'd replace classes for one week in the school year and bring in public speakers to lead workshops on racial justice and feminism awareness. We really did work hard. We really did try to figure out how to pull this off—within one school year. We made calls to organizations. We wrote to leaders in the community around Boston and Lawrence and Lowell and began negotiations to try to pay for them to come speak. But it was a lot to organize, a lot to manage, and we were all only seventeen and we only had a few months to try to get this all pulled together. . . .

And it didn't happen. All we were able to do was get the administration to commit to creating some scholarships for nonwhite students (which, even at that time, we knew was worth taking a very critical look at).

We didn't pull off the week of awareness. We didn't even get tangible proof of the scholarships. We had nothing to hold in our hands and say, *We did this.*

All of us in the club were seniors, and when we graduated, it was over. The club vanished. We felt like we'd accomplished nothing. We felt like we'd failed.

Or so I thought.

And my now-self is shaking his head at my then-self.

Because what I didn't know then, but what I know now, is that seeds grow.

And, like I said, sometimes you don't always see the results of your work.

Sometimes you plant seeds, but you're not there to see what it looks like when they push through the ground and rise into the air, green and vibrant, bending toward the sun with life.

Nothing you do is too small. Water, after all, can wear down and split rock—it just takes enough of it, all those tiny drops working together, not giving up, to slice through stone.

How do I know TASC's seeds took root? Because my younger brother also went to my high school. He started after I'd already graduated, but one day he called me up.

"Hey, B, that club you started? That week of awareness you wanted?" (I was listening. My heart kicked into quicker rhythm.)

"Yeah?"

"They're doing it. Some teachers picked up where you left off. They have this whole week set aside now. The Week of Awareness."

Holy @#&%?! Really?

Yup. Turned out that the year after I graduated, a couple teachers were inspired by the work we students had done and dedicated themselves to making it become a reality. (Quick shout-out to those kinds of teachers!) They pushed the administration to build that "week of awareness" into the school calendar. Well, at first it was just a day, sure. For a couple years they set aside one day a year for all the students to break out of their regular classes and attend workshops about social consciousness: about racism and white privilege, about toxic masculinity and feminism; about LGTBQ+ pride.

But then that day grew into a couple days . . .

And then that grew . . .

And the year my brother graduated, it became a whole week of awareness—just as we'd planned seven years earlier.

But then that grew too!

Or, rather, it morphed. It evolved. It became something even better than what we had planned, even better than what we had imagined. The whole day of awareness, week of awareness thing stopped altogether.

Wait, what? Oh no!

No, wait. Oh, yes!

Yes! Exactly. Because what happened was, we'd set something in motion that more people could begin to think about and analyze . . . and make much better. The school dumped the original concept because they realized they shouldn't be setting aside *one week* a year for the community to be thinking about racism and white privilege—they should be thinking about it the *whole year*, every day, in all their regular classes, in their sports program (remember that school chant?), in the whole attitude and life of the school. It meant changing the curriculum, it meant redesigning the admissions policies and hiring practices for teachers, it meant redefining what "community service" meant and looked like. It meant placing different priorities in all the materials they printed about the school.

Is it perfect? No. Far from it.

But is it better? I think so.

Now, is this all thanks to our little TASC club? No. The work of hundreds of people made this happen—thousands, really, when you think about all the students in the community who engaged in the effort and took it seriously. It was thousands of people.

But we planted the seed. And though we weren't there to watch it grow, it grew . . . and grew and grew and grew.

This is worth repeating: Never feel like what you are doing is too small or doesn't matter. Because imagine what you could grow if you choose to stand up and speak out and get involved.

Yusuf simply stood and asked a question. And because he did, he worked his way so deeply into Jason's heart that Jason later wrote and published a poem about Yusuf that tons of people have read. He worked his way so deeply into my heart too, so that later I called around until I could get him on the phone and hear more of his story, and print his speech in this book, so that you could hear the song of his heart as clearly and powerfully as I did.

What might grow if you sit down and write a letter to one of your congresspeople? Sure, it might be one of thousands landing on their desk, but what if they quote from it when they make a speech and that speech makes it on to the nightly news, makes it into the hearts of people watching at home?

Never feel like what you might do won't matter.

You could gather some friends and start a club and see what happens when it grows. . . .

But remember, white people don't need to take action *for* people of the Global Majority. No one needs, no one is looking for, a white savior. The point isn't to take action so we get credit for it, either. We also don't want to do something only once or twice, then forget about it like we're a "responsibility tourist."

Taking action for racial justice really has to become a way of life. A 24/7 commitment. It's about trying to *live* as much as possible in pursuit of racial justice in solidarity with people of the Global Majority.

Because right now, as long as there continues to be racial injustice, our society is broken. If we work to be a part of mending it, it helps us all. Or, as Martin Luther King Jr. said, "No one is free until we are all free." And that better future is possible, is absolutely possible, but only through a commitment (not a wish, not a desire, not even a hope), a full-hearted commitment, to working toward it.

And the thing is, throughout our country's history, as long as there has been this racial injustice, there have been people who've believed that a better future, a more racially just future, *is* possible, and they *committed to working* toward it . . . many, many people of the Global Majority and many white people, too.

So when you, as a white person, act with care and courage and commitment, *alongside* people of the Global Majority in this pursuit of racial justice, you are not alone. You join those who have come before you, white people who have, as best as possible, tried to live and work toward racial justice in solidarity with people of the Global Majority.

People like:

- **John Brown**, who, at only twelve years old, became a determined and ardent abolitionist and who, as he got older, worked with the Underground Railroad to help escaping enslaved people on their way to freedom, even fought side by side with Black people in a number of enslaved people's revolts across the country.

- **Mary White Ovington** and **Moorfield Storey**, a white woman and white man who worked in partnership with Black leaders W. E. B. Du Bois and Ida B. Wells to cofound the National Association for the Advancement of Colored People (NAACP).

- **Jack Greenberg**, who argued alongside Thurgood Marshall in the landmark Supreme Court case *Brown v. Board of Education* and who became the only white legal counselor for the NAACP Legal Defense Fund (now the Legal Defense and Educational Fund).

- **Anne McCarty Braden**, who fought racist real estate practices, tried to organize other white southerners like herself to join the civil rights movement, and worked closely with activists Rosa Parks and Ella Baker in the 1950s and '60s.

- **Joan C. Browning**, who, as a young college student, began volunteering with SNCC (Student Nonviolent Coordinating Committee, a civil rights organization) and participated in a variety of sit-ins and demonstrations throughout the state of Georgia.

- **Robert F. Kennedy**, who marched and worked with Dolores Huerta and Cesar Chavez in support of Latinx labor rights and the United Farm Workers movement.

- The long list of **Catholic nuns**, **Jewish rabbis**, and myriad **Christian ministers** who marched alongside John Lewis and Martin Luther King Jr. in support of civil rights.

- And so, so many more . . .

Although the history of racism and white privilege reaches back to the founding of our country, so too does the history of white people who *chose* instead to *pursue racial justice by working in solidarity with people of the Global Majority*.

Knowing that, think about this:

Today 71 percent of white people in America believe racism is a problem in our country—*71 percent*! Since we know that white privilege is racism, that also means that 71 percent of white Americans should believe that our own white privilege is a problem in our country as well. Right?

So now . . .

Imagine if all 71 percent of us *choose to join that history*, join the ranks of the Bobby Kennedys who *chose to listen* to people of the Global Majority when they spoke about the reality of racism, the Anne McCarty Bradens who *chose to work* with people of the Global Majority to not only fight the effects of racism in people's lives, but also to enhance and improve the lives of everyone in their communities.

What might our country look like then?

This is exactly the history the white students who stood in the lobby of the school in Brooklyn in solidarity with the students of the Global Majority were a part of! And not only them. This is the history you can also be a part of.

This is the future you could be a part of too.

It's a way of life, a commitment, reaching from history and into tomorrow by the work other young people around the country are doing today:

- Like the young woman in Sacramento who told me she was finding other young people on social media with whom to organize a coordinated Black Lives Matter rally in different cities across the country, even though they'd never met in person.
- Like the young people Jason and I met in Baltimore who held a "die-in" in their school cafeteria and forced their whole community to have a public conversation about racial justice.

- Like the students I met in Ohio who were taking on the sexism of their school's dress code through a series of social media posts.
- Like the student in Virginia who took his time on stage at a creative-writing competition to simply read out loud a list of things invented by Black Americans, from the gas mask to home security systems to Cascade dishwashing detergent to a specialized process for eye surgery, and other things important to the mostly white audience in the gym.
- Like the students I met in Boise, Idaho, who were writing letters to their state senators, asking them to make public statements that spoke out against the last president's racist comments about immigrants from Mexico and all over Central and South America.
- Like the students I met in Alaska and Colorado and Michigan and Nevada and New Hampshire and South Carolina and Florida and Georgia and Texas and all over the whole country, who shared with me what they cared about and why and who asked me how they could get more involved.

For those of us who are white, we can't escape being white and living with white privilege—we are part of that group. But *how* we live with this, what we choose to do about it, whether we commit to act toward more racial justice in solidarity with people of the Global Majority—*this all plays a vital role in who we are as individuals.*

So, yes. Hell yes.
Now it's time to take action!
Join that tradition and be part of shaping that future.
Show up. Speak out.
Do something.
You can.

You must.

Author's Note

I felt conflicted when I set out to write this book. Writing about race, racism, and white privilege, as a white person, is complicated. Partly because as soon as I write about it, my voice takes on that authorial voice of, well . . . *authority*. And I'm not an authority on race, racism, and white privilege in America. I'm someone working to learn more, and in writing about it, my hope is that sharing my process of working on it will be helpful for other people, white people in particular, in their efforts to learn more too.

What makes that authorial voice even more complicated, however, is that it takes up space. It says, "Hey, listen to me, please." And frankly, there have been so many people of the Global Majority speaking about this for so long, and so many voices of the Global Majority who have not yet been given the chance to share their wisdom. But likewise, I've heard so many people of the Global Majority asking white people to get more involved—to listen more, learn more, and to speak up more about racism and white privilege—and I do not want to dodge that call I've heard so loud and clear.

So the spirit of writing this book is not to take on a position of authority, but rather to acknowledge that I have listened, and will continue to listen, and to also take a risk and try to join a conversation that has been led by people of the Global Majority and has been happening for a long time. I'm trying to add a voice to the long list of writers and thinkers and scholars and activists and parents and colleagues and students and classmates and other individuals and organizations who have shaped my own thinking and perspective and, more importantly, have been driving this conversation about race and racism in America.

I've tried to acknowledge and include as many of those sources as I could in the list that follows: "Some People I Listened to and Learned from Who Influenced the Writing of This Book." And I encourage all readers of this book to read and seek out the sources listed there, particularly those written by writers of the Global Majority, and to seek out others not listed there as well. Maybe some of those sources are voices in your own community; for example, classmates, teachers, and other people of the Global Majority whose experience and wisdom may not have yet gotten enough "mic time."

But the complications I've been thinking about while writing this book also run deeper. It isn't only about mic time on the public stage. It's also about who gets to be on the public stage in the first place. Have I worked hard to become an author and educator? Absolutely. But as I've described in this book, I've also had enormous advantages that have given me more access to this public platform than many other people, particularly because of racism and white privilege.

To be blunt, it is also about money, access, and resources, and so to that end, though it is just a start, I want to make sure that any money I earn from this book also supports organizations empowering young people who have not had the resources, access, opportunities, and privileges I had growing up. To that end, I am donating 10 percent of all my earnings from this book to a number of youth empowerment programs across the country. And in the same way I encourage readers of this book to read and listen and learn from the sources listed in my "Some People I Listened to and Learned from" list, I also encourage readers of this book to think about the ways we can all reallocate money, and additional resources, to opportunities that empower young people. I invite you to do your part to invest in the structural changes necessary to create more equitable access to opportunities for all young people, and in particular, those who have traditionally been shortchanged in ways people like me have been overly advantaged.

And lastly, I know this book is only a part of a much larger commitment to live in a way that pursues more racial justice in our communities, our cities, and our country. And to buoy that commitment, I look to Bettina Love's wisdom as she outlines the difference between an ally and a co-conspirator (thank you, Joanna Ho, for pointing me here: vimeo.com/502300589), and I hope I can work harder at choosing to be a co-conspirator more often.

Acknowledgments

Acknowledging each and every person who has helped me write this book feels like trying to count the stars in the night sky—the beauty lies not only in each singular burst, but also in the bewildering magnitude of their aggregate. I'm grateful for the vast community of people who have influenced me in some way in the conceiving and writing of this book, and there are a few individuals I'd particularly like to thank.

First and foremost, to Rob Weisbach, who sent that first email ("What do you think?")—all love to you, always!

To Caitlyn Dlouhy, who found a disorganized mess of ideas on her doorstep and co-whittled it into the instrument I hope it can be—forever and ever thank you for helping me find my voice. Thank you, thank you, thank you for the hours, the energy, and your wisdom.

And to the rest of my S&S family: Carlo Péan, Justin Chanda, Anne Zafian, Jon Anderson, Lisa Moraleda, Lauren Hoffman, Chrissy Noh, Anna Jarzab, Dan Potash, Elizabeth Blake-Linn, Jeannie Ng, Cindy Nixon, Michelle Leo and the entire Ed & Library team—thank you for charging down this path with me. I only wish I could gather you around the family table and cook you all the biggest thank-you dinner ever.

To the friends, colleagues, and profoundly generous

writers and educators whose wisdom and insight shaped and reshaped my heart, my thinking, and my words, thank you for your time, patience, and energy for this book, and more importantly for your dedication to the belief and the work you always put in to reimagining and rebuilding our world for the better: Samira Ahmed, Olivia A. Cole, Sarah Fleming, Adam Gidwitz, Joanna Ho, Minh Lê, Cornelius Minor, Julie Murphy, Keith Newvine, Ellen Oh, Randy Ribay, Julia Torres, Renée Watson, and Phil Bildner, David Byrnes, Dhonielle Clayton, David Burr Gerrard, Andrew Hume, and Olugbemisola Rhuday-Perkovich—I really do love you all.

To the friends, colleagues, and thoroughly courageous and compassionate human beings whose real life experiences, wisdom, and spirit are the heartbeat of so many of the stories shared in this book: Beverly Billie (Taos and Acoma Pueblos, New Mexico), Randy Clancy, Tatesha Clark, Will Gilyard, Natasha Goddard, Elena Jaime, Nicole Swentzell (Kewa, Santa Domingo Pueblo, New Mexico), Jordina Coleman (and the entire Cheverus community) Yusuf Isaacs, and Mingus Daniels-Taylor—the work of trying to do justice to all that you have graciously shared with me is not limited to this book; I am there for you always.

Early drafts and sections of this book were developed as part of the Lower Manhattan Cultural Council's Arts Residency program (LMCC.net), and I'd like to particularly thank Bora Kim and Sophie Lam for their encouragement, support, and insight, and Asiya Wadud for a conversation that turned a corner in my thinking and set so much of this book in motion.

In my own life as an educator, this book is unimaginable

without the entire network of friends and colleagues and family in my former life at the Calhoun School (I miss you all so much!). Thank you, each of you, for your creativity and dedication to young people, and most especially to the incomparably life-affirming Hilary North. Thank you also to the cornerstones of my current life at the Solstice MFA program, Meg Kearny, Quintin Collins, Beth Little, and the whole team.

And while there have been so many people over the last fifteen years in my career as an educator, and more recently, as an author, too, whose intelligence and empathy and humanity inform these pages, in addition to those mentioned above, I am especially grateful to Elizabeth Acevedo; Laurie Halse Anderson; David Arnold; Jenn Baker; Sam Bloom (and Eric Carpenter, Ernie Cox, and Patrick Gall); Rose Brock; Allie Jane Bruce; Erica Corbin; Christina Dorr; Katie Freeman; John Gentile; Lamar Giles; Afton Gilyard; Alex Gino; Jenny Han; Nina Harmande; Jillian Heise; Jess Huang; Yahdon Israel; Tiffany Jackson; Dana Alison Levy; Nick Mancusi; Meg Medina; Daniel José Older; Debbie Reese; Steve Rosenstein; Chris Ross; Adam Silvera; Nic Stone; Namrata Tripathi; Morika Tsujimura; Benny Vásquez; Anshu Wahi; Jasmine Warga; Corey Whaley; Ashley Woodfolk; and Jeff Zenter. And, of course, everybody at the Hotel Bar who had to listen to me gripe—you know who you are. I appreciate you all more than there's room here to gush.

But whether it was over bagels before our early morning phone calls, backstage between presentations, over shrimp etouffee with loved ones, or just sitting quietly around your mother's kitchen table, this book lives and breathes with the air of so many of our conversations and travels together, Jason Reynolds. Thank you for your tenderhearted introduction; thank you for the kick in the pants to put this book in motion; thank you for those early, early talks as we walked the rainy streets of Portland; and thank you for all the laughter and joy and honesty and anger and sadness and silliness and celebration that is friendship that becomes family. Love you, man. With you, always, to the end.

And thank you to my family, Heide Lange and John Chaffee, Garima Prasai and Joshua Chaffee, Trish and Niall Kiely, and especially my mother, Maryanne Kiely, who've had to listen to me twist and untwist myself again and again as I worked, and whose love and support buoy me in work and in life—and an extra special thank-you to my grandmother Jane Kiely, who reminded me of how Solomon asked God for a listening heart, and gave shape to me as a writer and person. Love you all! But this book literally wouldn't have materialized at all without the dedication, patience, sharp thinking, and immeasurable support from my father, Tom Kiely—love you, Dad; I think we ended up having this *other talk* after all, didn't we?

And most importantly, my life has no meaning without its center—Jessie and Finn, I love you, I love you, I love you.

Endnotes

1: Bottle of Nesquik, Bottle of Long Since Forgotten
pp. 1–6: In order to construct the narrative of Jordan Davis's experience and life, I relied on the following sources:

"The Death of Jordan Davis: A Family's Search for Justice," *The Takeaway*, produced by Amber Hall, June 13, 2015, wnycstudios.org/podcasts/takeaway/episodes/death-jordan-davis-familys-search-justice.

McLaughlin, Eliott C., and John Couwels, "Michael Dunn Found Guilty of 1st-Degree Murder in Loud-Music Trial," CNN, October 1, 2014, cnn.com/2014/10/01/justice/michael-dunn-loud-music-verdict.

News Service of Florida staff, "Florida Supreme Court Rejects Appeal for Man Convicted of Killing Jacksonville Teen Jordan Davis," Action News Jax, June 22, 2020, actionnewsjax.com/news/local/duval-county/florida-supreme-court-rejects-appeal-man-convicted-killing-jacksonville-teen-jordan-davis/POMLXEIUY5BBBK5JSXK4ZYHTXA.

2: Two Americas
p. 11: "George Zimmerman was acquitted . . ." George Zimmerman was found not guilty in the trial for his killing of Trayvon Martin, in part due to the particular details of

Florida's "Stand Your Ground" statute in his claim of firing his gun in self-defense. And the legal complications of the case are explained more thoroughly here: Carter, Chelsea J., and Holly Yan, "Why This Verdict? Five Things That Led to Zimmerman's Acquittal," CNN, last updated July 15, 2013, cnn.com/2013/07/14/us/zimmerman-why-this-verdict.

p. 12: "There are two Americas . . ." The transcript for Dr. Martin Luther King Jr.'s March 14, 1968 speech at Grosse Point High School, in which he described these two Americas, can be found here: King Jr., Martin Luther, "The Other America," Grosse Point High School Society, n.d., gphistorical.org/mlk/mlkspeech/index.htm.

3: So What Is This Talk I Never Got?

pp. 18–19: In order to learn more about who George Floyd was, I relied on the following sources:

Fox 9 Staff, "Who Was George Floyd?" Fox9, last updated March 19, 2021, fox9.com/news/who-was-george-floyd.

Henao, Luis Andres, Nomaan Merchant, Juan Lozano, and Adam Geller, "A Long Look at the Complicated Life of George Floyd," *The Chicago Tribune*, June 11, 2020, chicagotribune.com/nation-world/ct-nw-life-of-george -floyd-biography-20200611-cxmlynpyvjczpbe6izfduzwv54 -story.html.

Levenson, Eric, "Former Officer Knelt on George Floyd for 9 Minutes and 29 Seconds—Not Infamous 8:46," CNN, last updated March 30, 2021, cnn.com/2021/03/29/us/ george-floyd-timing-929-846/index.html.

Hill, Evan, et al., "How George Floyd Was Killed in

Police Custody," *New York Times*, May 31, 2020, nytimes
.com/2020/05/31/us/george-floyd-investigation.html.

p. 22: "As too many Black families . . ." For more stories like
my friend's, watch this short documentary from the *New York
Times*: Gandbhir, Geeta, and Blair Foster, "A Conversation
with My Black Son," *New York Times*, March 17, 2015, nytimes
.com/video/opinion/100000003575589/a-conversation
-with-my-black-son.html.

p. 23: "Living as a white person . . ." Claudia Rankine dis-
cusses what she means by "white living" as a term to use
instead of "white privilege" from these following sources:

Hirsch, Afua, "Claudia Rankine: By White Privilege I
Mean the Ability to Stay Alive," *The Guardian*, September 5,
2020, theguardian.com/books/2020sep/05/claudia-rankine
-by-white-privilege-i-mean-the-ability-to-stay-alive.

Haber, Leigh, "Claudia Rankine's *Just Us* Prompts a
Conversation All Americans Need to Have," Oprah Daily,
August 4, 2020, oprahmag.com/entertainment/books/
a33481843/claudia-rankine-interview-just-us-american
-conversation.

4: How I Tell a Story

p. 31: "Black boys and young men . . ." "Young Black Men
Are 21 Times as Likely as Their White Peers to be Killed by
Police," Equal Justice Initiative, October, 14, 2014, eji.org/
news/study-shows-young-Black-men-21-times-more-likely
-to-be-killed-by-police.

Gabrielson, Ryan, Eric Sagara, and Ryann Grochowski
Jones, "Deadly Force, in Black and White," ProPublica,

October 10, 2014, propublica.org/article/deadly-force-in
-black-and-white.

p. 31: "Black people comprise about . . ." Criminal Justice Fact
Sheet, NAACP, n.d., naacp.org/criminal-justice-fact-sheet.

Lopez, German, "There Are Huge Racial Disparities in
How US Police Use Force," Vox, last updated November
14, 2018, vox.com/identities/2016/8/13/17938186/police
-shootings-killings-racism-racial-disparities.

p. 31: "Black people are nearly twice . . ." Swaine, Jon, Oliver
Laughland, and Jamiles Lartey, "Black Americans Killed by
Police Twice as Likely to Be Unarmed as White People," *The
Guardian*, June 1, 2015, theguardian.com/us-news/2015/
jun/01/black-americans-killed-by-police-analysis.

p. 31: "Indigenous people are more . . ." Hansen, Elise, "The
Forgotten Minority in Police Shootings," CNN, last updated
November 13, 2017, cnn.com/2017/11/10/us/native-lives
-matter/index.html.

pp. 31–32: "In New York City in 2017 . . ." ACLU of New
York, Stop-and-Frisk Data, NYCLU, n.d., nyclu.org/en/stop
-and-frisk-data.

p. 32: "And yet white people . . ." Balko, Radley, "There's
Overwhelming Evidence That the Criminal Justice System Is
Racist. Here's the Proof," *The Washington Post*, June 10, 2020,
washingtonpost.com/graphics/2020/opinions/systemic
-racism-police-evidence-criminal-justice-system.

p. 32: "In Arizona the results . . ." ACLU of Arizona, "Driving
While Black or Brown: An Analysis of Racial Profiling in
Arizona," ACLU, April 2008, leephillipslaw.com/articles/
RacialProfiling.pdf.

5: White Boy

p. 41: "Vincent Chin was a . . ." Little, Becky, "How the 1982 Murder of Vincent Chin Ignited a Push for Asian American Rights," History, May 5, 2020, history.com/news/vincent -chin-murder-asian-american-rights.

Wang, Frances Kai-Hwa, "Who Is Vincent Chin? The History and Relevance of a 1982 Killing," NBC News, last updated June 15, 2017, nbcnews.com/news/asian-america/ who-vincent-chin-history-relevance-1982-killing-n771291.

p. 42: "long history of racism . . ." De Leon, Adrian, "The Long History of Racism Against Asian Americans in the U.S.," PBS, April 9, 2020, pbs.org/newshour/nation/ the-long-history-of-racism-against-asian-americans-in -the-u-s.

"Japanese-American Internment During World War II," National Archives, last updated March 17, 2020, archives .gov/education/lessons/japanese-relocation.

p. 44: "Asian American women twice . . ." Chen, Shawna, "AAPI Women More Than Twice as Likely to Report Hate Incidents as Men, Report Finds," Axios, March 16, 2021, axios.com/anti-asian-hate-report-89ff12fb-f4ef-4eea-946a -c755e786f043.html?utm_source=newsletter&utm_ medium=email&utm_campaign=newsletter_axiospm &stream=top.

pp. 46–47: "Motel 6 recently had to . . ." Jacobs, Julia, "Motel 6 Agrees to Pay $8.9 million to Settle Claims It Helped ICE Arrest Guests," *New York Times*, November 6, 2018, nytimes .com/2018/11/06/us/motel-6-lawsuit-ice-settlement.html.

6: Chicken-and-Egg Problem . . . Solved!

pp. 51–52: "all human beings across . . ." Goodman, Alan, "Race Is Real, But It's Not Genetic," *Discover Magazine*, June 25, 2020, discovermagazine.com/planet-earth/race-is-real-but-its-not-genetic.

p. 52: "call it a 'social fact.'. . ." Gannon, Megan, "Race Is a Social Construct, Scientists Argue," LiveScience, *Scientific American*, February 5, 2016, scientificamerican.com/article/race-is-a-social-construct-scientists-argue/#:~:text=More%20than%20100%20years%20ago,between%20different%20populations%20of%20people.

Bonilla-Silva, Eduardo, "The Essential Social Fact of Race," *American Sociological Review*, vol. 64, no. 6 (December 1999), pp. 899–906, jstor.org/stable/2657410?seq=1.

p. 53: "Race is the child of . . ." Coates, Ta-Nehisi, *Between the World and Me* (New York: Penguin Random House, 2015), p. 7.

p. 54: "A person considered 'Black' . . ." Onwuachi-Willig, Angela, "Race and Racial Identity Are Social Constructs." *New York Times*, last updated September 6, 2016, nytimes.com/roomfordebate/2015/06/16/how-fluid-is-racial-identity/race-and-racial-identity-are-social-constructs.

p. 54: "people of Mexican birth . . ." Desmond-Harris, Jenée, "11 Ways Race Isn't Real," Vox, October 10, 2014, vox.com/2014/10/10/6943461/race-social-construct-origins-census.

p. 54: "racial categorization for immigrants . . ." Varathan, Preeti, "For One Year, All the South Asians in the US Were Considered 'White,'" Quartz India, September 2, 2017,

qz.com/india/1066287/for-one-year-all-the-south-asians
-in-the-us-were-considered-white.

p. 54: "there was debate about . . ." Desmond-Harris, Jenée, "11 Ways Race Isn't Real," Vox, October 10, 2014, vox .com/2014/10/10/6943461/race-social-construct-origins -census.

p. 54: "people from Germany, Ireland . . ." Desmond-Harris, Jenée, "11 Ways Race Isn't Real," Vox, October 10, 2014, vox .com/2014/10/10/6943461/race-social-construct-origins- census.

p. 55: "A study showed that . . ." Chou, Vivian, and Daniel Utter, "How Science and Genetics Are Reshaping the Race Debate of the 21st Century," *Science in the News*, Harvard University, the Graduate School of Arts and Sciences, April 17, 2017, sitn.hms.harvard.edu/flash/2017/science-genetics -reshaping-race-debate-21st-century.

p. 55: "'Ethnic groups in Western Africa . . .'" Kendi, Ibram X, *How to Be An Antiracist*, New York: One World, 2019, p. 53.

7: Cheating to Win

p. 62: "July 2 is actually . . ." "Did You Know . . . Independence Day Should Actually Be July 2," National Archives, June 1, 2005, archives.gov/press/press-releases/2005/nr05-83.html.

pp. 64–66: "Time line of Policies . . ." I found the stats and other useful information for this time line from multiple sources:

"Go Deeper: Race Timeline," *Race – The Power of an Illusion*, PBS, pbs.org/race/000_About/002_03_c-godeeper.htm.

Merritt, Keri Leigh,"Land and the Roots of African-

American Poverty," *Aeon*, March 11, 2016, aeon.co/ideas/land-and-the-roots-of-african-american-poverty.

"The Immigration Act of 1924 (The Johnson-Reed Act)," Office of the Historian, n.d., history.state.gov/milestones/1921-1936/immigration-act#:~:text=The%20quota%20provided%20immigration%20visas,completely%20excluded%20immigrants%20from%20Asia.

p. 67: "constructing a cage around . . ." Matthews, Dylan, "Woodrow Wilson Was Extremely Racist—Even by the Standards of His Time," Vox, November 20, 2015, vox.com/policy-and-politics/2015/11/20/9766896/woodrow-wilson-racist.

p. 69: "what *systemic white privilege* . . ." These statistics are all taken from the following book: DiAngelo, Robin, *White Fragility: Why It's So Hard for White People to Talk About Racism* (Boston: Beacon Press, 2018).

p. 70: "white people are only . . ." Frey, William H., "The Nation Is Diversifying Even Faster Than Predicted, According to New Census Data," Brookings Institution, July 1, 2020, brookings.edu/research/new-census-data-shows-the-nation-is-diversifying-even-faster-than-predicted.

Frey, William H., "Less Than Half of US Children Under 15 Are White, Census Shows," Brookings Institution, June 24, 2019, brookings.edu/research/less-than-half-of-us-children-under-15-are-white-census-shows.

8: How History Lives in the Present

p. 72: "benefits provided by the . . ." History.com, "G.I. Bill," History, last updated June 7, 2019, history.com/

topics/world-war-ii/gi-bill#:~:text=Officially%20the%20
Servicemen's%20Readjustment%20Act,attending%20
college%20or%20trade%20schools.

p. 76: "Florida in the 2000 . . ." Berman, Ari, "How the
2000 Election in Florida Led to a New Wave of Voter
Disenfranchisement," *The Nation*, July 28, 2015, thenation.
com/article/archive/how-the-2000-election-in-florida-led
-to-a-new-wave-of-voter-disenfranchisement.

Palast, Greg, "1 Million Black Votes Didn't Count in
the 2000 Presidential Election/It's Not Too Hard to Get
Your Vote Lost—If Some Politicians Want It to Be Lost,"
The San Francisco Chronicle, June 20, 2004, sfgate.com/
opinion/article/1-million-black-votes-didn-t-count-in
-the-2000-2747895.php.

pp. 76–77: "Wisconsin in the 2016 . . ." Berman, Ari,
"Wisconsin's Voter-ID Law Suppressed 200,000 Votes in
2016 (Trump Won by 22,748)," *The Nation*, May 9, 2017,
thenation.com/article/archive/wisconsins-voter-id-law
-suppressed-200000-votes-trump-won-by-23000.

pp. 77–78: "Georgia in the 2018 . . ." Durkin, Erin, "GOP
Candidate Improperly Purged 340,000 from Georgia Voter
Rolls, Investigation Claims," *The Guardian*, October 19, 2018,
theguardian.com/us-news/2018/oct/19/georgia-governor-
race-voter-suppression-brian-kemp.

Lockhart, P.R., "The Lawsuit Challenging Georgia's Entire
Elections System, Explained," Vox, last updated May 30,
2019, vox.com/policy-and-politics/2018/11/30/18118264/
georgia-election-lawsuit-voter-suppression-abrams-kemp
-race.

Shah, Khushbu, "'Textbook Voter Suppression': Georgia's Bitter Election a Battle Years in the Making," *The Guardian*, November 10, 2018, theguardian.com/us-news/2018/nov/10/georgia-election-recount-stacey-abrams-brian-kemp.

Caputo, Angela, Geoff Hing, and Johnny Kauffman, "After the Purge: How a Massive Voter Purge in Georgia Affected the 2018 Election," AMP Reports, October 29, 2019, apmreports.org/story/2019/10/29/georgia-voting-registration-records-removed.

p. 80: "in the late 1800s companies . . ." Blakemore, Erin, "The Brutal History of Anti-Latino Discrimination in America," History, last updated August 29, 2018, history.com/news/the-brutal-history-of-anti-latino-discrimination-in-america?li_source=LI&li_medium=m2m-rcw-history.

p. 80: "in a terrifying raid . . ." Blakemore, Erin, "The Brutal History of Anti-Latino Discrimination in America," History, last updated August 29, 2018, history.com/news/the-brutal-history-of-anti-latino-discrimination-in-america?li_source=LI&li_medium=m2m-rcw-history.

p. 80: "US government forcibly removed . . ." Blakemore, Erin, "The Brutal History of Anti-Latino Discrimination in America." History.com, last updated August 29, 2018, history.com/news/the-brutal-history-of-anti-latino-discrimination-in-america?li_source=LI&li_medium=m2m-rcw-history.

p. 81: "Latinx people were denied . . ." Gamboa, Suzanne, "Racism, Not Lack of Assimilation, Is the Real Problem Facing Latinos in America," NBC News, February 26, 2019,

nbcnews.com/news/latino/racism-not-lack-assimilation
-real-problem-facing-latinos-america-n974021.

p. 81: "Abercrombie & Fitch was accused . . ." "Abercrombie
& Fitch Employment Discrimination," NAACP Legal
Defense and Education Fund, March 17, 2006, naacpldf.org/
case-issue/abercrombie-fitch-employment-discrimination.

Greenhouse, Steven, "Abercrombie & Fitch Bias Case Is
Settled," *New York Times*, November 17, 2004, nytimes.com/
2004/11/17/us/abercrombie-fitch-bias-case-is-settled.html.

p. 81: "'You'd be surprised!' . . ." Arana, Marie, "A
History of Anti-Hispanic Bigotry in the United States,"
The Washington Post, August 9, 2019, washingtonpost.
com/outlook/a-history-of-anti-hispanic-bigotry-in-the
-united-states/2019/08/09/5ceaacba-b9f2-11e9-b3b4
-2bb69e8c4e39_story.html.

9: The Entire System Is Rigged

pp. 84–85: "close to eighteen million . . ." "Facts About Child
Hunger in America," No Kid Hungry, n.d., nokidhungry.org/
who-we-are/hunger-facts.

p. 85: I learned about food insecurity statistics and find-
ings from the following source: Bauer, Lauren, "About 14
Million Children in the US Are Not Getting Enough to Eat,"
Brookings Institution, July 9, 2020, brookings.edu/blog/
up-front/2020/07/09/about-14-million-children-in-the-us
-are-not-getting-enough-to-eat.

p. 86: "Students who have regular . . ." Seaton, Jaimie,
"Reading, Writing, and Hunger: More Than 13 Million
Kids in This Country Go to School Hungry," *The Washington*

Post, March 9, 2017, washingtonpost.com/news/parenting/ wp/2017/03/09/reading-writing-and-hunger-more-than -13-million-kids-in-this-country-go-to-school-hungry.

p. 87: I found information on systemic injustice in incarceration rates from: Kerby, Sophia, "The Top 10 Most Startling Facts About People of Color and Criminal Justice in the United States," Center for American Progress, March 13, 2012, americanprogress.org/issues/race/ news/2012/03/13/11351/the-top-10-most-startling-facts -about-people-of-color-and-criminal-justice-in-the-united -states.

pp. 87–88: For systemic injustice in education, I found the following sources helpful:

Meatto, Keith, "Still Separate, Still Unequal: Teaching about School Segregation and Educational Inequality," *New York Times*, May 2, 2019, nytimes.com/2019/05/02/ learning/lesson-plans/still-separate-still-unequal-teaching -about-school-segregation-and-educational-inequality.html.

Meckler, Laura, "Report Finds $23 Billion Racial Funding Gap for Schools," *The Washington Post*, February 25, 2019, washingtonpost.com/local/education/report-finds-23-billion -racial-funding-gap-for-schools/2019/02/25/d562b704 -3915-11e9-a06c-3ec8ed509d15_story.html.

Hsieh, Steven, "14 Disturbing Stats About Racial Inequality in American Public Schools," *The Nation*, March 21, 2014, thenation.com/article/archive/14-disturbing-stats-about -racial-inequality-american-public-schools.

p. 88: The following sources were helpful in finding out info on systemic injustice in business:

Hanks, Angela, Danyelle Solomon, and Christian E. Weller, "Systemic Inequality: How America's Structural Racism Helped Create the Black-White Wealth Gap," Center for American Progress, February 21, 2018, americanprogress .org/issues/race/reports/2018/02/21/447051/systematic -inequality.

Williams, Dima, "A Look at Housing Inequality and Racism in the U.S.," *Forbes*, June 3, 2020, forbes.com/ sites/dimawilliams/2020/06/03/in-light-of-george-floyd -protests-a-look-at-housing-inequality/?sh=7cab59ff39ef.

pp. 88–89: For systemic injustice in healthcare, I found the following sources informative:

Gelrud Shiro, Ariel, and Richard V. Reeves, "Latinos Often Lack Access to Healthcare and Have Poor Health Outcomes. Here's How We Can Change That," Brookings Institution, September 25, 2020, brookings.edu/blog/ how-we-rise/2020/09/25/latinos-often-lack-access-to -healthcare-and-have-poor-health-outcomes-heres-how-we -can-change-that.

Hathaway, Bill, "New Analysis Quantifies Risk of COVID-19 to Racial, Ethnic Minorities," *Yale News*, May 19, 2020, news.yale.edu/2020/05/19/new-analysis-quantifies-risk -covid-19-racial-ethnic-minorities.

Morales, Laurel, "Many Native Americans Can't Get Clean Water, Report Finds," *Morning Edition*, NPR, November 18, 2019, npr.org/2019/11/18/779821510/many-native -americans-cant-get-clean-water-report-finds.

p. 89: I found information on systemic injustice in housing from these sources:

Lake, Jaboa, "The Pandemic Has Exacerbated Housing Instability for Renters of Color," Center for American Progress, October 30, 2020, americanprogress.org/issues/poverty/ reports/2020/10/30/492606/pandemic-exacerbated -housing-instability-renters-color.

Solomon, Danyelle, Connor Maxwell, and Abril Castro, "Systemic Inequality: Displacement, Exclusion, and Segregation," Center for American Progress, August 7, 2019, americanprogress.org/issues/race/reports/ 2019/08/07/472617/systemic-inequality-displacement -exclusion-segregation.

Perry, Andre M., Jonathan Rothwell, and David Harshbarger, "The Devaluation of Assets in Black Neighborhoods," The Brookings Institution, November 27, 2018, brookings.edu/research/devaluation-of-assets-in -black-neighborhoods.

pp. 90–91: For the discussion on the effects of the Clinton era "tough on crime" policies, see: Alexander, Michelle, *The New Jim Crow: Mass Incarceration in the Age of Colorblindness* (New York: The New Press, 2011), pp. 56–57.

10: Ninja Runs

p. 111: "Real estate agents in Long . . ." Pfeiffer, Sacha, and Stefano Kotsonis, "*Newsday* Investigation Reveals Sweeping Real Estate Discrimination on Long Island," *On Point*, WBUR, November 25, 2019, wbur.org/onpoint/2019/11/25/ newsday-long-island-real-estate-investigation.

pp. 111–12: "signed an executive order . . ." Shear, Michael D., and Helene Cooper, "Trump Bars Refugees and Citizens of 7

Muslim Countries," *New York Times*, January 27, 2017, nytimes
.com/2017/01/27/us/politics/trump-syrian-refugees.html.

11: Hard Look in the Mirror

pp. 117–18: "Two white people who . . ." The list that follows emerges from the form and idea Peggy McIntosh outlined in her famous essay:

McIntosh, Peggy, "White Privilege: Unpacking the Invisible Knapsack," *Peace and Freedom* (July/August 1989), pp. 10–12.

Interruption

p. 125: "more than fifteen hundred . . ." Graham, David A., "The Stubborn Persistence of Confederate Monuments," *The Atlantic*, April 26, 2016, theatlantic.com/politics/archive/2016/04/the-stubborn-persistence-of-confederate-monuments/479751.

p. 126: Richard Allen: "Richard Allen, 1760–1831," Africans in America: Part 3: 1791–1831, PBS, n.d., pbs.org/wgbh/aia/part3/3p97.html.

p. 126: Mary Ellen Pleasant: Chambers, Veronica, "Overlooked." *New York Times*, January 31, 2019, nytimes.com/interactive/2019/obituaries/mary-ellen-pleasant-overlooked.html.

p. 126: Mary Fields: Blakemore, Erin, "Meet Stagecoach Mary, the Daring Black Pioneer Who Protected Wild West Stagecoaches," History.com, last updated January 28, 2021, history.com/news/meet-stagecoach-mary-the-daring-black-pioneer-who-protected-wild-west-stagecoaches.

pp. 126–27: Lewis Latimer: Biography.com editors, "Lewis Howard Latimer," Biography.com, last updated January 7, 2021, biography.com/inventor/lewis-howard-latimer.

p. 127: Marcario García: History.com editors, "Marcario García Becomes First Mexican National to Receive U.S. Medal of Honor," History.com, last updated August 20, 2020, history.com/this-day-in-history/marcario-garcia-first -mexican-national-to-receive-us-medal-of-honor.

pp. 127–28: Dr. Kazue Togasaki: "Dr. Kazue Togasaki," National Park Service, n.d., nps.gov/people/dr-kazuetogasaki.htm.

p. 128: Kiyoshi Kuromiya: "Life of Kiyoshi Kuromiya: From Selma Marcher to AIDS Activist," NBCNews.com, last updated March 7, 2015, nbcnews.com/storyline/ selma-50th-anniversary/selma-marcher-aids-activist -life-steven-kuromiya-n318876.

p. 128: Sylvia Mendez: Jennings, Lisa, "The End of the 'Mexican School,'" Hispanic Business.com, May 2004, web. archive.org/web/20061029130350/http://www.hispanic business.com/news/newsbyid.asp?id=15976&cat= Magazine&more=/magazine.

p. 128: Albert Baez: Nelson, Valerie J., "Albert V. Baez, 94; Physicist, Father of Joan Baez," *Los Angeles Times*, March 23, 2007, latimes.com/archives/la-xpm-2007-mar-23-me -baez23-story.html.

p. 128: Bayard Rustin: Gates Jr., Henry Louis, "Who Designed the March on Washington?" "The African Americans: Many Rivers to Cross," PBS.org, n.d., pbs.org/wnet/african-americans -many-rivers-to-cross/history/100-amazing-facts/who -designed-the-march-on-washington.

p. 129: Dolores Huerta: Godoy, Maria, "Dolores Huerta: The Civil Rights Icon Who Showed Farmworkers 'Sí Se Puede,'" "The Salt," NPR.org, September 17, 2017, npr.org/sections/thesalt/2017/09/17/551490281/dolores-huerta-the-civil-rights-icon-who-showed-farmworkers-si-se-puede.

p. 129: Larry Itliong: Romasanta, Gayle. "Why It Is Important to Know the Story of Filipino-American Larry Itliong," Smithsonianmag.com, July 24, 2019, smithsonianmag.com/smithsonian-institution/why-it-is-important-know-story-filipino-american-larry-itliong-180972696.

p. 129: Marsha P. Johnson: Maxouris, Christina. "Marsha P. Johnson, a Black Transgender Woman, Was Central Figure in the Gay Liberation Movement," CNN, last updated June 26, 2019, cnn.com/2019/06/26/us/marsha-p-johnson-biography.

p. 129: Wilma Mankiller: Brando, Elizabeth, "Wilma Mankiller," National Wome's History Museum, 2021, womenshistory.org/education-resources/biographies/wilma-mankiller.

p. 129: Mohammad S. Hamdani: Fenner, Austin, "Muslim Cop Cadet Mourned," *New York Daily News*, April 6, 2002, nydailynews.com/archives/news/muslim-cadet-mourned-article-1.488329.

p. 130: Mae Jemison: Scott, Rachel. "1st Black Female Astronaut in Space Offers Advice to Young Girls," ABCNews.go.com, May 23, 2018, abcnews.go.com/GMA/Culture/black-female-astronaut-space-offers-advice-young-girls/story?id=55351207.

p. 130: LaDonna Harris: NAP Staff, "Indigenous Women

Rise: Women's March on Washington," Nativephilanthropy
.org, January 10, 2017, nativephilanthropy.org/2017/01/10/
indigenous-women-rise-womens-march-washington.

p. 130: Fazlur Rahman Khan: Sommerlad, Joe. "Fazlur
Rahman Khan: Why Is This Skyscraper Architect So
Important?" *Independent*, April 3, 2017, independent.co.uk/
arts-entertainment/architecture/fazlur-rahman-khan
-skycraper-architect-engineer-google-doodle-willis-tower-
john-hancock-bangladeshi-american-a7663926.html.

p. 130: Faisal Alam: Ogles, Jacob, "21 LGBT Muslims Who
Are Changing the World," *The Advocate*, December 20, 2016,
advocate.com/religion/2016/12/20/21-lgbt-muslims-who
-are-changing-world.

p. 130: Dr. David Ho: Grayce West, Melanie, "New York City
Invests in Rapid Covid-19 Test to Aid Economic Recovery,"
The Wall Street Journal, February 28, 2021, wsj.com/articles/
new-york-city-invests-in-rapid-covid-19-test-to-aid
-economic-recovery-11614528000.

12: What Bullying Looks Like . . . to a Whole Community

p. 136: "One place in particular . . ." Aizenman, Nurith, "Trump
Wishes We Had More Immigrants from Norway. Turns Out
We Once Did," *Goats and Soda*, NPR, January 12, 2018,
npr.org/sections/goatsandsoda/2018/01/12/577673191/
trump-wishes-we-had-more-immigrants-from-norway
-turns-out-we-once-did.

pp. 138–39: "Like this domino effect" Fuchs, Chris, "Reported
Anti-Muslim Hate Incidents, Rhetoric Rose in Year after

Election, Report Finds," NBC News, February 1, 2018, nbcnews.com/news/asian-america/reported-anti-muslim-hate-incidents-rhetoric-rose-year-after-election-n843671.

pp. 141–42: "My colleague's story wasn't . . ." Anderson, Curt, "FBI: Hate Crimes Vs. Muslims Rise," AP News, November 25, 2002, apnews.com/article/5e249fb6e4dc 184720e3428c9d0bd046.

p. 142: "about 'flying while Muslim' . . ." Editorial Board, "Flying While Muslim Is Not a Crime," The Washington Post, August 8, 2016, washingtonpost.com/opinions/flying -while-muslim-is-not-a-crime/2016/08/08/7b568a02-5dac -11e6-9d2f-b1a3564181a1_story.html.

14: Well, Actually, Hang on a Second . . . Step Back
p. 150: "people who do not identify as white . . ." "Frequently Asked Questions," PGM ONE, n.d., pgmone .org/contact#:~:text=support%20my%20registration %3F-,What%20does%20%22people%20of%20the%20 global%20majority%22%20mean%3F,80%25%20of%20 the%20world's%20population.

16: Messing Up . . . and Listening
pp. 162–63: "Here's what he said." Korver, Kyle, "Privileged," *The Players' Tribune*, April 8, 2019, https://www.theplayers tribune.com/articles/kyle-korver-utah-jazz-nba.

18: Listening . . . without Getting Defensive
p. 172: "to grant interviews to people . . ." Gerdeman, Dina, "Minorities Who 'Whiten' Job Resumes Get More

Interviews," *Working Knowledge*, Harvard Business School, May 17, 2017, hbswk.hbs.edu/item/minorities-who-whiten -job-resumes-get-more-interviews.

Francis, David R., "Employers' Replies to Racial Names," *The Digest*, National Bureau of Economic Research, no. 9 (September 2003), nber.org/digest/sep03/employers -replies-racial-names.

Burnett, Jane, "Strong Job Candidates with Foreign Names Miss Out on Job Interviews, Study Shows," The Ladders, February 24, 2017, theladders.com/career-advice/ study-ethnic-sounding-name-employers-fewer-calls-back.

p. 173: Miami University enrollment by race: "First-Year Class Profile (Fall 2019)," Office of Institutional Diversity & Inclusion, Miami University, n.d., miamioh.edu/diversity-inclusion/data-reports/enrollment/index.html.

p. 193: " It was great." Wiggington Greene, Catherine, and André Robert Lee. *I'm Not Racist . . . Am I?* Pointe Made Films. 2014.

19: Listening . . . and Believing

p. 180: "students of the Global . . ." Frey, William H., "Less Than Half of US Children Under 15 Are White, Census Shows," Brookings Institution, June 24, 2019, brookings. edu/research/less-than-half-of-us-children-under-15-are -white-census-shows.

p. 187: "admitted to killing Emmett . . ." Huie, William Bradford, "The Shocking Story of Approved Killing in Mississippi," *Look* (January 1956). Reprinted in "The Murder of Emmett Till: Killers' Confession," *American Experience*, PBS,

n.d., pbs.org/wgbh/americanexperience/features/till-killers
-confession.

p. 187: "also admitted that she . . ." Pérez-Peña, Richard,
"Woman Linked to 1955 Emmett Till Murder Tells Historian
Her Claims Were False," *New York Times*, January 27, 2017,
nytimes.com/2017/01/27/us/emmett-till-lynching-carolyn
-bryant-donham.html.

p. 189: "And again in the 5,712 cases . . ." Lucchesi, Annita
(Southern Cheyenne), and Abigail Echo-Hawk (Pawnee),
"Missing and Murdered Indigenous Women and Girls," Our
Bodies, Our Stories series, Urban Indian Health Institute,
Seattle Indian Health Board, 2018, uihi.org/wp-content/
uploads/2018/11/Missing-and-Murdered-Indigenous
-Women-and-Girls-Report.pdf.

p. 189: "More than 6,600 hate . . ." Yancey-Bragg,
N'dea, "A Historic Surge: Anti-Asian American hate
incidents continue to skyrocket despite public awareness
campaign," *USA Today*, May 6, 2021, usatoday.com/story/
news/nation/2021/05/06/racism-us-anti-asian-hate-grows
-despite-biden-speech-activism/4969692001.

20: Taking Action

p. 213: "71 percent of white . . ." Galston, William A., "When
It Comes to Public Opinion on Race, It's Not 1968 Anymore,"
Brookings Institution, June 22, 2020, brookings.edu/blog/fixgov/
2020/06/22/when-it-comes-to-public-opinion-on-race-its
-not-1968-anymore.

SOME PEOPLE I LISTENED TO AND LEARNED FROM WHO INFLUENCED THE WRITING OF THIS BOOK

Books and Periodicals

Alexander, Michelle. *The New Jim Crow: Mass Incarceration in the Age of Colorblindness*. New York: The New Press, 2011.

Anderson, Carol. *White Rage: The Unspoken Truth of Our Racial Divide*. New York: Bloomsbury, 2016.

Billings, David. *Deep Denial: The Persistence of White Supremacy in United States History and Life*. Roselle, NJ: Crandall, Dostie & Douglass Books, Inc., 2016.

Biss, Eula. "White Debt." *New York Times*. December 6, 2015.

Coates, Ta-Nehisi. *Between the World and Me*. New York: Penguin Random House, 2015.

———. "The Case for Reparations." *The Atlantic*. June 2014.

Davis, Angela Y. *Women, Race & Class*. New York: Vintage Books, 1983.

DiAngelo, Robin. *White Fragility: Why It's So Hard for White People to Talk About Racism*. Boston: Beacon Press, 2018.

Dunbar-Ortiz, Roxanne, Jean Mendoza, and Debbie Reese.

An Indigenous Peoples' History of the United States for Young People. Boston: Beacon Press, 2019.

Hannah-Jones, Nikole, and The New York Times Magazine, eds. *The 1619 Project.* (Series). New York: New York Times, 2019.

Eddo-Lodge, Reni. *Why I'm No Longer Talking to White People About Race.* New York: Bloomsbury, 2017.

Higginbotham, Anastasia. *Not My Idea: A Book About Whiteness.* New York: Dottier Press, 2018.

Hudson, Wade, and Cheryl Willis Hudson, eds. *The Talk: Conversations about Race, Love & Truth.* New York: Penguin Random House, 2020.

Ignatiev, Noel. *How the Irish Became White.* New York: Routledge, 1995.

Iyer, Deepa. *We Too Sing America: South Asian, Arab, Muslim, and Sikh Immigrants Shape Our Multiracial Future.* New York: The New Press, 2015.

Jewell, Tiffany. *This Book Is Anti-Racist: 20 Lessons on How to Wake Up, Take Action, and Do the Work.* Minneapolis: Frances Lincoln Children's Books, 2020.

Joseph, Frederick. *The Black Friend: On Being a Better White Person.* Somerville, MA: Candlewick Press, 2020.

Kendi, Ibram X. *How to Be an Antiracist*. New York: Penguin Random House, 2019.

Kivel, Paul. *Uprooting Racism: How White People Can Work for Racial Justice*. Gabriola Island, British Columbia: New Society Publishers, 1996.

Love, Bettina. *We Want to Do More Than Survive: Abolitionist Teaching and the Pursuit of Educational Freedom*. Boston: Beacon Press, 2020.

McIntosh, Peggy. "White Privilege: Unpacking the Invisible Knapsack." *Peace and Freedom*. July/August 1989, pp. 10–12.

Minor, Cornelius. *We Got This: Equity, Access, and the Quest to Be Who Our Students Need Us to Be*. Portsmouth: Heinemann, 2018.

Morrison, Toni. *Playing in the Dark: Whiteness and the Literary Imagination*. Reprint, New York: Knopf Doubleday, 1993.

Nobles, Melissa. *Shades of Citizenship: Race and the Census in Modern Politics*. Stanford: Stanford University Press, 2000.

Olou, Ijeoma. *So You Want to Talk About Race*. New York: Seal Press, 2018.

Ortiz, Paul. *An African American and Latinx History of the United States*. Boston: Beacon Press, 2018.

Painter, Nell Irvin. *The History of White People*. New York: W.W. Norton & Company, 2010.

Rankine, Claudia. *Just Us: An American Conversation*. Minneapolis: Graywolf Press, 2020.

Reynolds, Jason, and Ibram X. Kendi. *Stamped: Racism, Antiracism, and You: A Remix of the National Book Award–winning Stamped from the Beginning*. New York: Little, Brown and Company, 2020.

Saad, Layla F. *Me and White Supremacy: Combat Racism, Change the World, and Become a Good Ancestor*. Reissue, Naperville, IL: Sourcebooks, 2020.

Wise, Tim. *White Like Me: Reflections on Race from a Privileged Son*, 2nd ed. Berkeley: Soft Skull Press, 2008.

Websites and Blogs

Abolitionist Teaching Network (a myriad of resources and virtual presentations available here): abolitionistteachingnetwork.org

Angry Asian Man (blog): blog.angryasianman.com

The Brown Bookshelf (blog): thebrownbookshelf.com

The CARLE Institute (racial justice in education organization): carleinstitute.com

Center for Racial Justice in Education (a myriad of resources and workshops available here): centerracialjustice.org

CrazyQuiltEdi (blog): crazyquiltedi.blog

The Players' Tribune (for Kyle Korver's April 8, 2019 article, "Privileged"): theplayerstribune.com/articles/kyle-korver-utah-jazz-nba

Latinxs in Kid Lit (blog): latinosinkidlit.com

Learning for Justice (a myriad of resources): learningforjustice.org

People's Institute for Survival and Beyond (another myriad of resources and workshops available here): pisab.org

Reading While White (blog): readingwhilewhite.blogspot.com

American Indians in Children's Literature (blog): american indiansinchildrensliterature.blogspot.com

We Need Diverse Books (a myriad of resources available here too): diversebooks.org

Podcasts

Joffe-Walt, Chana, reporter. *Nice White Parents*, produced by Julie Snyder, Serial Productions.

Mckesson, DeRay, host. *Pod Save the People*, Crooked Media.